What to do
When the
Bubble Pops

ALSO BY HARRY S. DENT, JR.

Be Your Own Boss

What to do When the Bubble Pops

Personal and Business Strategies for the Coming Economic Winter

HARRY S. DENT, JR.

MEDIA

Published 2020 by Gildan Media LLC
aka G&D Media
www.GandDmedia.com

Front cover design by David Rheinhardt of Pyrographx

Interior design by Meghan Day Healey of Story Horse, LLC

Library of Congress Cataloging-in-Publication Data is available upon request

ISBN: 978-1-7225-0201-0

10   9   8   7   6   5   4   3   2   1

Contents

Introduction

I've been forecasting trends in the economy since the late eighties. My forecasts are based not only on in-depth research into demographics, economic cycles, and technologies, but also on practical business experience.

I have a different approach to the economy, and it's something you can understand. We're not talking about complex, academic, economic principles. We're talking about the predictable things people, businesses, and technologies do as they move in the economy. I have predicted some major economic shifts that nobody else saw. In the late eighties, I foresaw the collapse of Japan and its real-estate and stock bubble. From the early nineties on, I foresaw the greatest boom in history for the rest of the world, especially Europe and the United States.

For decades now, we've been seeing a roller-coaster economy. This was not the way the economy looked after World War II, in the fifties and sixties. It started to change in the seventies—recession after recession, along with the greatest inflation rates in history and the OPEC oil embargo. As I'll show later, the baby boom was the largest generation in history, both here in the United States and around the world, and in the seventies, it was just hitting the economy for the first time. Young people are expensive, and they're the biggest cause of inflation. (I'm going to explain a lot of things like this in common-sense terms.) Emerging countries are famous for having higher inflation rates. That's because the populations are younger: they have much higher proportions of young people. So the seventies were the first time you could start to sense that something was different.

Now we're in a whole new economy, with new technologies. The baby boomers created a great expense to be educated and then incorporated in the workforce, but they also brought in new technologies—the information revolution. Those technologies further accelerated the globalization revolution. That's what has caused such dramatic growth and volatility.

The next thing we saw were the recessions of 1980–82 and the highest unemployment since the Great Depression. Next thing you know, the stock market's booming. Next thing after that, in 1987, the stock market crashes 40 percent, for the most part in two weeks, 20 percent in one day. What caused that? That was the first sign of bubbling stock markets, the first since the Roaring Twenties. During the entire boom from 1942 to 1968, we had never seen a 40 percent correction in stocks. It was a much more moderate, predictable, and less volatile stock market. The largest corrections were more like 20 percent. So in the eighties, again, something was different, and it was the baby boomers.

Then in the early nineties, we saw the first savings and loan crisis. As I've already pointed out, we saw the collapse of Japan. There was an absolute stock market rout and the biggest bursting of a real-estate bubble we've seen in modern times. That happened supposedly out of nowhere. People were calling it a black swan. This was not a black swan. Otherwise I couldn't have predicted it in 1988 and 89. What was causing this was the baby boom in Japan, which came and peaked much earlier than it did in the U.S.

In the nineties, we saw the great tech bubble and the great crash to follow. Everybody was flipping technology stocks from late 1994 into early 2000. It was the greatest stock run we'd seen since 1925–29. What was causing this? Radical new technologies, the most powerful in history, but again, by this massive baby-boom generation. You get greater growth, greater bubbles, and greater crashes.

We finally recovered from the tech crash. We had another bubble, not as dramatic, from late 2002 to late 2007. It suddenly crashed in 2008 and early 2009, and we saw the deepest recession since the Great Depression. It's called the Great Financial Crisis or the Great Recession. Actually, it started to look like a depression, which I was predicting at the time.

Yet another time we saw a bubble burst, and central banks, beginning with the Federal Reserve, started to print money. They were throwing trillions of dollars into the economy to stop the entire banking system from failing, as it did in the early thirties. Governments always lower interest rates. They always start building dams and doing things to make business better, but this was something new. They'd never before said, "We're going to print a dollar for every dollar the economy or the stock market drops. We're just going to fill in the holes with dollars." That's called *quantitative easing*, but it's really printing money out of thin air. That ignited another bubble, and that bubble is peaking coming into 2020.

I'll show you why that the next crash is going to be worse than the last one. The next economic crisis is going to be more like the Great Depression. I'll show you why that happens. The Great Depression was not a black swan. Nor was the collapse of Japan in the early nineties. You can predict these are things if you understand what actually drives the economy.

To summarize, this whole boom, along with the inflation that preceded it, is more pervasive, more dynamic, and more global than we've ever seen. When we get a downturn, we don't just go down; everybody goes down. And this boom has been foolishly extended by central banks around the world, which propose to treat the greatest debt bubble in history with more debt. You don't treat a debt crisis with more debt any more than you deal with a drug habit with more heroin. A ten-year-old could figure this out.

In this book I'm going to show you in simple and human terms why all of this is occurring, what's driving it, and where we're going from here. First, you have to understand how we got here. My goal is to educate you enough so that you can take clear and decisive action to protect your assets and your family and will also see the dramatic opportunities ahead. I'm going to show you that this will be a once-in-a-lifetime sale on financial and business assets.

The real-estate bubble in the United States, the stock bubble around the world—even the bubbles in education and health care, which nobody can afford anymore—are all going to come to an end, but it's going to take a great crisis, what I call a Great Reset to do that.

This is a time where you can create extreme wealth. First, you have to protect your assets. You have to get out of the bubble. Don't listen to people who say this is not a bubble. Extreme wealth comes from the people who see this coming. In the 1930s, the last time we had what I call a winter season like this, companies like General Motors passed their competitors, never to be caught for decades after that. Their gains in market share gains paid off almost forever.

In the late twenties, Joseph Kennedy, a smart investor, sold his stocks at the top of the bubble, when shoeshine boys were starting to tell him what stocks to buy. He knew something was wrong. Later he bought the stocks and businesses back at 10 cents on the dollar. That's extreme wealth. That's how you take advantage of a major shift in the economy of this kind.

This bubble was created by fundamental reasons. Governments, central banks, Wall Street, and other players and special interests made it much worse. There's only one way for bubbles to end—to burst and allow a major restructuring and deleveraging of debt and financial asset bubbles to bring things back to reality. You're going to see huge opportunities, but most importantly, you're going to see simple ways to protect your wealth now.

Most people out there are preaching ideology. This is no ideology. I'm telling you the truth about what's happening and why. You have to be convinced enough again to take decisive action now.

Before I get into all of this, let me give you a summary of my background and past predictions. I was an accidental economist. As an undergraduate, I dropped my major in economics, because after the third course, I didn't see the practical, real-life applications. I realized that nobody can understand this stuff. Unlike scientists (most of the time), economists disagree when they're looking at the same data. In fact, they're famous for reminding us that nobody can predict the future. Really? I've been predicting the future for three decades now.

The most important trends are predictable. You can see those trends and how they're going to impact your life, your family, your business, and your investments over the rest of your lifetime. That's where our research is focused.

When I got to Harvard Business School, I learned some important concepts about life cycles in business. All technologies, all products, and all industries go through four stages and seasons, just as we do in our life cycle. You have to have a different strategy for each stage and season. (I'll talk about this in chapters 6 and 7.)

This is why businesses succeed and then suddenly fail. People say, "What happened? What did they do wrong?" They were doing what was already working, but that doesn't work when the stages and seasons change.

When I got out of Harvard, I got a super job at Bain & Company, one of the three leading global consulting companies for business strategies to Fortune 100 companies. I'm a young Harvard MBA. I'm consulting at the highest levels to major companies, and we're making major changes exactly for the reasons I've mentioned. Companies did something that succeeded in one stage of the economy or their industry life cycle. Then things switched, but they kept going in the same direction and didn't have a clue why they were failing. It takes somebody who is objective and understands these stages and cycles to help them.

I did that for a couple of years, but it wasn't my calling. Bain & Company was great, I learned a lot in two years, but I was still working with large companies that take forever to make decisions and change. (Of course, they were much more bureaucratic back then, in the early eighties, before the great restructuring brought about by the information age.) So I started working with new ventures. I'm not talking high-tech, like Apple computers. I'm talking about everyday ventures.

Most of these companies were focused on consumer areas, and a lot of them were start-ups, so I did the same kind of stage and business strategy consulting I would do to Fortune 100 companies—and more affordably; I had to take a cut in pay at first, for small businesses. But I loved entrepreneurs, and I loved working with smaller businesses. If I'm sitting with an entrepreneur and I get them to see something, they're going to be making the change thirty minutes from now, or the next morning. I really liked that, and I did it for many years. This is where I discovered the power of demographics.

The Fortune 100 companies were appealing to the old trends and the old generation—I call them the Bob Hope generation. The new companies were growing in niche markets precisely because they were using new technologies, but more importantly, they were appealing to the up-and-coming, more innovative baby boomers, who were setting new trends.

Not only did I key into the new technologies that were driving our economy, but most importantly, I realized I had to study these baby boomers. I realized that this was not a normal generation. They were more creative, more entrepreneurial, more radically innovative, but most importantly, there was a massive number of them. When you look at the size of their birth wave—and it's been extended by increased immigration—they are like a ten-foot wave compared to the Bob Hope generation before them, which was a three-foot wave. The millennial or echo-boom generation following the boomers are more like a five-foot wave.

The baby boom was a disruptive generation. All the volatility we've seen since the seventies can only be explained by the baby-boom generation, because they supercharge everything.

In the eighties, while I was consulting to entrepreneurial businesses, I developed real-life, step-by-step indicators based on people and business life cycles in order to predict how consumers and business innovation drive our economic progress and cycles. It's not the superficial government reactions and policies, which the economists follow. That is like the tip of the iceberg; it's not the 80 percent below the surface that nobody sees.

Governments do not drive our economy. They react first to the trends set by business, which in turn is responding to consumers. The government reacts last. You don't see the future by looking at government. Yes, if they're going to print a bunch of money, it's going to cause a short-term stimulus, but that does not create long-term trends, and government's going to learn this very painfully.

Since the early eighties, just one or two key demographic indicators, which I'll discuss later, have enabled me to foresee economic cycles, such the crash in Japan in the nineties. In 1988–89, I kept saying that Japan was going to see a twelve- to fourteen-year downturn: real-estate bubbles and stock bubbles were going to burst. I also foresaw the great boom in the rest of the world, especially Europe and the United States. I don't know anybody else who predicted those two things simultaneously. There were a few people, like Sir John Templeton, who foresaw one—the boom of the nineties—but very few saw both of these coming.

I'm rarely wrong when I call for a major change. Sometimes I can be a little early, and sometimes I can miss the magnitude, but when I say Japan's going to collapse, they're going to collapse. When I say we're going to have a great boom, we have a great boom.

I also predicted the recession and the first real-estate downturn in the United States in the early nineties. I said that we were going to have a two-year slowdown and then a strong boom. When the economy got going and even exceeded our forecast, I was calling for a Dow of 10,000 by the early 2000s. It went even higher than that, peaking in March 2000. People were saying I was crazy for predicting that strong a boom when the Dow was only at 2,000 to 3,000. Actually, I underestimated the boom, and I realized that I had been leaving out the immigrants. After that point, I started including them in my analysis.

In February 2000, we predicted that the Internet bubble was bursting, and in March the NASDAQ and tech bubble did start to burst. When this market bottomed in October 2002, we had a whole bunch of short-term indicators that said, "OK, this is done. If you don't buy stocks here, you won't likely get another chance like this for a while." That's exactly when they took off, and we had the next bubble into 2007. For twenty years, since the late eighties, I'd been warning that the baby-boom spending wave would peak roughly by late 2007; then we would go into another generational downturn, as we saw from 1969 to 1982 with the Bob Hope generation, and from 1930 to 1942 with the Henry Ford generation before that.

Then, I said, we'd go into a longer-term downturn, and in 2008, we got the Great Recession. If it hadn't been for the massive money printing in the following years, it would have developed into a major depression. We're still going to see this. You can't beat Mother Nature simply by printing money forever.

Here's one thing I missed. Back in the early twentieth century, they had two tech bubbles: one that peaked in late 1919 and crashed in the early twenties, and a second one from 1922 to 1929. When that 2002 bottom hit, I expected a repeat of the two earlier ones. I expected the next bubble from late 2002 to 2007 to be as large as or larger than the tech bubble before it. I was predicting a Dow of 32,000 to 35,000 into 2007. That didn't happen. It only went up to about half that.

That's when I found a new cycle, and I'll look at it later.

I can be wrong about things, but I'm not wrong about major shifts. That's why I'm asking you to take my comments seriously. I have no axes to grind, no special interests. I don't work for a brokerage firm or a bank. I don't have to be bullish or bearish. I just call it as I see it. That independence alone gives me an edge that most people don't have.

Chapter One

The Amazing Power of Demographics

People throughout history—politicians, major analysts, and economists—almost never see bubbles, even though if you step back and look, they're obviously there. Nothing could be more obvious than that a market that rises exponentially for five years or more and then bursts, because nothing can grow exponentially without bursting.

Now we're in 2020. Nine out of ten analysts I debate on TV still say this is not a bubble. I'm going to show you that this *is* a bubble, and the number-one thing you have to do is protect yourself: get out of this bubble, because when they burst, they burst dramatically.

Let me start with the most important principle for forecasting that I have found. It came from working with entrepreneurs and studying the emerging baby boom in the 1980s. I call it the amazing power of demographics. Individuals aren't predictable, but large groups of people are highly predictable. We know when generations of people will spend money. Spending grows dramatically from the time that people enter the workforce, get their starter jobs, and buy their starter cars and homes to when their family cycle matures. At that point, they're earning the most in their career and spending the most money.

When do people enter the workforce? On average at age 20. They spend the most money at age 46 for the boomers; it's 47 currently for the millennials. They plateau well after that and then drop off dramatically. Their kids leave the nest and they save for retirement. They have their highest net worth at age 64. When they get into retirement—at age 63 on average—they spend down their wealth.

This is how the baby boom reshaped our economy. They followed the Bob Hope generation, whose spending was declining in spending in the 1970s, specifically from 1969 to 1982. You know how many stock crashes and recessions we had in that period? The stock crash and recession of 1970, then the stock crash and recession of 1973 and 1974, which was the worst stock crash and one of the deepest recessions we had had for a long time. In 1980–82, at the end of the bottom of that cycle, we had stock crashes and the deepest recession. This was not a black swan. It was the last generation fading before the baby boomers emerged in the workforce to start to replace their parents' spending power.

Again, there were three major cycles in the last century. There was the Henry Ford generation from the late 1800s into 1929. At that point the stock market didn't only peak because it was in a bubble: it was the end of that generation's spending cycle. Unlike the baby boom, that generation was not characterized by high birth rates. The boom was caused by massive immigration, at that time largely from Europe. If I were to track peak spending of those immigrants, I'd say, "You know what? The biggest peak would be 1929, then there'd be a crash. There'd be one more surge of immigrants into 1937 and there'd be a big stock rally there, followed by another crash." That's exactly what happened.

It was the same thing with the Bob Hope generation. They didn't fully enter the workforce until 1942. Their spending wave went into late 1968, and then we saw the series of stock crashes in the 1970s. It was a recessionary economy, surprisingly accompanied by high inflation rates.

I innovated this generational spending wave for the first time in 1988, discovering that a 46-year lag on the birth index would tell you when the economy's going to boom and bust. That is, if you look at the year of the peak birth rate for that generation and go forward 46 years, you will see the year of that generation's peak spending.

It took me another year to figure out that young people cause inflation. Parents have to raise kids at great expense: it costs $250,000 on average to raise a kid just through high school; you have to add much more if they go to college. Governments have to fund their education. That's a huge discretionary expense. It's all investment, all expense. When this generation enters the workforce, businesses have to give them office space, equipment, and training. It takes two and a half years after they enter the workforce for the new generation to start to produce more than they cost. That's why in 1989 I came up with the *inflation indicator*, a 2½-year lag on workforce growth.

This massive 10-foot wave of baby boomers caused inflation rates to go to unprecedented levels. If you go back all the way in the modern history of the United States or Europe, you will not see inflation rates as high and extended as we saw from the late sixties into the late seventies. Then that inflation bubble burst, and commodity prices—such as for oil and gold—went down with them in the early to mid-eighties. The next thing you know, we had a booming economy with falling inflation.

Again, that's the baby boomers. Workforce growth slowed, increasing productivity and spending, as this new generation in their massive numbers started becoming contributors to the economies rather than takers. Young people take. They need investment. They're not supposed to be productive; they're supposed to learn. You learn, you earn, and then you return in your later years. That's exactly what demographics show.

Young people cause inflation because of their expense, but young people are also innovators. They come fresh; they look at things differently. They bring innovations, like personal computers. They bring new technologies and new entrepreneurial businesses.

The second wave is the spending wave. That's when we're raising our families, advancing in our careers, earning and spending more money. Again, there are dramatic differences between what a 20-year-old earns when entering the workforce and what people earn at their peak. It can be two to three times as much. When a whole generation does that, of course the economy would grow.

Governments will take credit for it, but it's not governments. I was predicting the greatest surge in the economy in the 1990s from the late eighties on, including government budget surpluses for the first time in decades as a result of a booming economy from baby boomers and the emergence of the kind of Internet technologies that were due to hit them. These things are more important than government policies.

Of course, it's not just a question of when people they spend or when they cost money. From cradle to grave, we focus on different things. When you're young, you need baby clothes and child care; you need apartments; then, as soon as you can afford it, you need a starter home. When your kids turn into testy teenagers and everybody needs more space, you buy your trade-up home. You want the kids way over there and you want to be way over here. That's when people buy McMansions. The starter homes come at age 31; the trade-up home at around age 41. That's why housing started to collapse before the broader economy did. It did that in the Roaring Twenties: housing peaked in 1925, but the economy didn't peak until 1930, then started to crash.

Again, we do predictable things from cradle to grave. Automobiles are a great example. That's one of the large durable-goods sectors that has held up after housing crashed and furniture slowed down. Watch this—from 2021 forward, automobiles are going to crash. Even if the economy didn't slow down, as I'm going to be predicting later on, automobiles would crash from natural factors, because people spend the most money on automobiles between age 53 and 64. Their kids have left the nest, and they don't need a minivan to cart them around anymore. The parents get a luxury car—a Lexus or a BMW—or a sports car or a pickup truck. This is when people spend the most: when they finally have discretionary income and they're not spending it all on the kids.

Then, of course, you can imagine spending on health care, vitamins, pharmaceuticals, nursing homes, and so on. From cradle to grave, I have hundreds of categories I can study now thanks to the information revolution. Governments like ours have consumer-expenditure surveys. They survey the spending of 5,000 families every year, even on things like potato chips. For the average family, spending on these peaks at age 42. It's not the parents that are eating the potato chips; it's the teenagers.

Cradle to grave, we can predict spending in hundreds of categories, so you as a business or an investor can see what's going to boom next and whether the economy's going up or not.

This broader slowdown and "winter season" that I've been forecasting from 2008 to 2023 is about to enter a second, much more ugly phase by early 2021 at the latest, but here are ten key sectors where baby boomers are going to spend more money than ever (although the economy may work against this to some degree).

1. The biggest is discretionary health care, wellness, and weight loss. Why *discretionary* health care? Medicare and Medicaid are going to get squeezed, because the government's promised much more than it can afford, with this massive baby-boom generation moving into retirement and claiming these benefits, while a smaller younger generation, less flush in income, is less able to support them. On the other hand, spending on discretionary health care—things that people spend their own money on—will go up. This includes everything from cosmetic surgery to wellness categories of all kinds, such as vitamins, diet aids, and weight loss. These things are going to boom more than ever. This is an area that you as an entrepreneur or an investor can start to look into.

2. What do older people do when their kids leave the nest? They travel. They first travel overseas to places like Europe, or Tahiti, or Thailand. That goes from about the late 40s to age

60; then it tapers off. Why? Travel is stressful. What people do next? They say, "Put me on a cruise ship, stuff me with food and booze, and I'll be happy. No customs, no jet lag." Spending here peaks at age 74; at that point people start to lose the energy to travel, and some of them start to die.

3. Health, life insurance, and financial planning. This is something people do when they're saving for retirement and into retirement. So these professions will do well even in a downturn.

4. Here's a surprise—recreational vehicles: RVs. If I were talking to a car dealer or salesman who's doing well, I would say, "You need to sell that car dealership, or you need to get into an RV dealership. Because the biggest surge is between ages 53 and 63, and that is still ahead for the baby boomers for the first half of the next decade."

5. Cruise ships, as a result of overseas travel.

6. Housing is going to contract, because the baby boomers are through buying their biggest

homes. But some people buy vacation homes into their late 40s, and there will be a second boom when this generation surges into their early to mid-60s.

As kids leave the nest, the parents want to do one of two things: either they downsize and move into a townhouse or condo closer to downtown, where there's entertainment and other amenities, or they want to move farther outwards, to quieter, more peaceful, and more affordable areas. When they get into their 70s and 80s, nursing homes will boom. Then, of course, the younger generation will be wanting starter homes and rentals. These sectors will do better.

7. Landscaping and home-maintenance services. Old people don't want to deal with these things, and it's not a convenience that costs a lot of money. People will pay for these services out of their own pockets.

8. Convenience stores and drugstores. We already see this in Japan, which is far ahead of us in its high proportion of old people to the general population. Older people don't want

to go to big grocery stores. They don't want to drive several extra miles. They'll go to convenience stores.

Older people also need a lot of pharmaceutical products. Pharmaceuticals peak at age 77; vitamins are on a similar cycle. Most of these things are absolutely necessary. You are not going to cut back on them. Besides, drugstores have become convenience stores. These sectors will do better than, say, grocery stores, where families shop to feed their kids.

9. Funeral homes and cremation services. I know this isn't a popular thing to do, but you should consider investing in these industries. If you're a real estate developer and find that nobody wants McMansions anymore, build funeral homes.

10. My favorite, and probably the sector with the highest growth rate for the longest period of time, is nursing homes and assisted-living facilities. Like funeral homes, these businesses need real estate. They need people to work in them and invest in them. This area is going to have high revenues.

Let me touch on another topic to round out this discussion. For any country, you can find the same lags for peak spending. In Europe, as well as Japan, South Korea, Singapore, and Taiwan, peak spending tends to occur when the generation peak is at age 47. In this country, we have more immigrants, who tend to live not quite as long and peak a little earlier in their spending. They cause us to peak a little earlier.

Using these figures, we were able to foresee the collapse of Japan. We were able to see that the United States would boom into late 2007, and Europe would boom a little longer into late 2011.

Of course I can't go into every single country, but let me talk about three groups of countries in the developed world.

The first category is *gainers*. These consist of seven small countries that have an echo boom, or millennial baby boom, that is larger than the baby boom. That's very rare. Those countries are small, so they're not going to tip the scales globally, but they'll be great places to move to or do business or invest in. Israel, Australia, Singapore, and New Zealand have high immigration. Switzerland has high immigration and is a safe haven. Sweden and Norway have higher birth rates, because they treat women very well. By the way, Australia, Switzerland, New Zealand, and Singapore attract very high-quality immigrants; that's even better. Even in the slowdown, these countries are going to be booming.

The second group of countries is larger, There are only five of them. I call them *sustainers*. These countries have had an echo boom that reaches more or less the same birth-rate levels as the baby boom. It's not as strong a trend: it's not a ten-foot wave, it's a five-foot wave, but they started from higher birth rates. These countries are the United States, Canada, France, the United Kingdom, and Denmark.

Now here's the bad news: most developed countries don't have substantial echo booms. As people become more affluent and located more in cities, they have fewer kids. This is even happening in emerging countries, but it's extreme in developed countries. We have countries like Japan and South Korea that have birth rates around 1.3 births per woman, whereas it takes 2.1 births just to sustain the population. (Actually, we're below that level in the U.S., but not by a lot, because of our immigrant populations.)

Most countries in the developed world are in this third category: *decliners*. Fourteen major countries are in this category. Japan is number one: it was the first country to age, and it is the fastest-aging country in the world. In the 1980s, when Japan and its stock market looked great, and they were taking over industries—buying Pebble Beach and properties in New York and London—we said that the Japanese were going down and we were going up.

Today Germany is in the same situation. The steepest decline in spending trends from 2018 to 2022 is in Germany, with slowing trends beyond that for decades. They are the next Japan. Everybody expects Germany to hold up the European Union. Good luck on that.

Portugal, Italy, Spain, and Greece are in trouble already. Imagine what will happen as their demographics get much weaker. Taiwan, South Korea, and East Asia are following Japan. South Korea is Japan on a 22-year lag. That's the difference between their peak in baby-boom births and Japan's. Neither country has immigration of any significance, so they're even easier to predict.

Austria is a Central European country that's very strong, and it's going to do well. Russia already has a declining workforce and even a declining life expectancy. The Netherlands is going to decline more than people think. So are Belgium and Finland. Finland is the one country in Scandinavia that has worsening demographic trends and is not a sustainer.

There is only one emerging country that has declining demographic trends: China. China is going to be the epicenter of the next global bust. Nobody else sees the great China bubble bursting, even though its growth rates are coming down dramatically already. Its low 6 percent growth rate in 2019 is forecast to be more like 5 percent in 2020. Wait until we see 2021.

There's one other factor that you need to understand, and I've seen this only in the last decade. When I first started studying demographics, there was a very clear peak in spending in the age 45 to 49 time frame, reaching the top at age 46. After the kids left the nest, spending dropped off dramatically. The biggest drop was at ages 50 to 54.

Now, having updating our demographic statistics with more detailed research, I see that the

50 to 54 category continues to spend. The peak is still 46, but the plateau continues. It's because the rich have gotten richer. There's the bubble boom, the advance of technologies, and the entrepreneurial revolution, where people are rewarded for higher risks, just as they are in Wall Street and financial investment.

The rich enter the workforce later. They go to school longer. They peak in spending later. Their kids go to school later. Their spending peaks when they are in their early to mid-50s. The wealthy, the top 20 percent, benefited from this bubble of quantitative easing and a continual rise in stock and real-estate values, because they own most of these assets. But they are going to stop spending dramatically in the next several years, and nobody's going to see that coming. Central banks won't be to do much more to prevent the 3-year great depression ahead—something we've been predicting for decades and especially in recent years. Yes, we have a once-in-a-lifetime great depression coming, and you'd better see it.

I've just given you an overview of the power of demographics. It's been especially important since World War II, when we saw the first broad middle-class generation emerge. Before that, we didn't have a broad middle class, in which every-body had strong incomes and could afford to mortgage a house over 30 years; very few people did. So in this period, the average person became more important.

I predicted that the Dow would to go to 32,000–35,000 by 2007. That didn't happen, even though I was right about the boom: earnings did well and the economy grew. Everything happened, except that the stock market didn't bubble up as much. I had to ask myself why. What was different from the Roaring Twenties, when the second bubble was even bigger?

I found that every 18 years, we get alternating geopolitical cycles—positive and then negative. First, everything in the world is hunky-dory: no major wars or embargoes. The last time that hap-pened was from 1983 to 2000. We had declining inflation. We had one 100-hour war with Iraq to kick them back into own their country after invading Kuwait, and then it was over. We didn't try to take over the country. We didn't try to bring in new leadership. We just defended our ally and got out. In 1998, we had one hedge fund collapse. The Russian ruble had a short crisis. That was it from 1983 to 2000.

What happened in 2001? You know—9/11. That changed everything. Ever since 2001, we've seen one geopolitical challenge and crisis after the next. We've had two failed wars in Iraq and Afghanistan—two expensive wars that only destabilized the region. I wish we could have helped those people, but we caused nothing but problems. Then we had the Arab Spring: one civil war after the next in Egypt, Tunisia, Libya, and Syria.

On top of that, Russia invaded Crimea and is pressuring Ukraine. Now you have extreme tensions between Western Europe and Russia, and between Russia and the United States. All of a sudden we have the Cold War coming back. Notice this, by the way: When did we have the Cold War and the Vietnam War, with rising inflation and the Middle East oil embargo? They happened in the previous adverse geopolitical cycle from late 1965 to late 1982. Again, it's approximately 18 years down and 18 years up.

The good news here is that this cycle bottoms around late 2019 to early 2020. The rising tensions with Iran, especially with Trump taking out its top general in January 2020, should be the culmination of all of the U.S. interventions.

Since 9/11 we've been seeing more civil wars and terrorism. Al Qaeda grew after that, even though we killed Osama bin Laden. ISIS came out of the instability in Iraq and Syria, and it's worse than Al Qaeda. Now we have this bigger threat than ever, along with continued acts of terrorism around the world. This cycle will slowly turn around in the years ahead, as the Cold War did in the early to mid-1980s, when Reagan started talking to Gorbachev. The Cold War faded, the Berlin Wall came down, and the Soviet Union fell in 1989–90. Things got better, and we had a hunky-dory time again into 2000.

This cycle does not greatly affect global growth, although of course it affects the countries that are having the conflicts and wars. This cycle affects military expenditures and similar things, but it does not have enormous impact on corporate earnings or revenues. It does, however, create higher perception of risk among businesspeople, especially investors. Therefore this cycle has its biggest impact on stock valuations. At the top of a geopolitical cycle, the price-to-earnings ratio tends to be double what it is at the bottom of an adverse one.

This cycle explained to me why the Dow didn't go to record highs, as it did in the previous bubble. The cycle was in its adverse phase, creating higher risk and uncertainty in the world. As a result, stocks didn't bubble up as much.

The geopolitical cycle and the demographic spending wave cycle in the United States don't converge (as they did from 1983 to 2000—the best part of the stock market, and the greatest bubble) again until 2023 to 2036. That'll be the next global boom. At that point we'll be seeing the next period of higher stock valuation.

My third major cycle is the *innovation cycle*. This is a broad productivity trend that improves business profits and wages. For decades, I've tried to line up the innovation cycle with the generation cycle, because, as I've said, young people are innovators. But as I studied history, I found that these two didn't quite line up. Instead I found that we have the highest productivity, the largest number of patent issuances, when powerful clusters of technologies emerge together— in the past, steamships and canals, railroads and telegraphs, automobiles, phones, and electricity. More recently, it's been personal computers, wireless phones, the Internet, broadband, and smartphones. Here it's a 45-year cycle. It's not a matter of when these things are invented; it's when they move into the mainstream, into everyday households. This is when the benefits from these innovations are at their highest.

To go back to the nineteenth century, the trend toward steamships and canals peaked in 1875. It dropped off dramatically as railroads emerged. At this point, railroads moved mainstream. Railroad revenues relative to the economy peaked in 1920—exactly 45 years later—and then tapered off.

The next wave, which came with the Bob Hope generation, emerged into niche markets in the Roaring Twenties: automobiles, electrical appliances. These items peaked around 1965. At that point about 80 percent of households had automobiles, and some had two. That wave of innovation started in the early 1900s and grew dramatically afterward. By 1965, it was fully mainstreamed, and then it leveled off for many years. By 1965, our whole interstate system was largely completed. There were similar peaks in ownership of TVs, radios, and other electrical appliances in 1965–66. These technologies started moving into urban areas and more afflu-ent households in the Roaring Twenties, but they didn't get to Homer Simpson until the 1950s and mid-1960s.

The latest innovation cycle of course started with personal computers. These emerged in the 1980s, to be joined by cell phones and smaller computing devices, but the Internet was the key critical application—the killer app. It emerged in the early to mid-1990s; by 2010, basically every-body was on the Internet. Today most people have smartphones; everybody has a cell phone.

Innovations such as email and Google have enabled us to take huge strides in productivity. I'm in the business of economic research. I used to have three full-time assistants. Now I have one. I can do most of the research myself just by Googling, and I can find things that neither my assistant nor I could have found before. It's unbe-lievable how these things have changed my busi-ness, and many others.

This innovation cycle is a broader indicator for timing booms and busts. When you combine it with demographic indicators, generational spending waves, and the geopolitical cycle, it will tell you when things are going to be a little better.

All three of these cycles pointed up at the same time, from 1988 (after the 1987 stock-market crash) into 2000. That's when the economy was the best; that's when stocks did the best; that's when we had the biggest bubble without massive money printing by the central bank. Everything had come together—baby boomers, innovation, and a wonderful geopolitical environment.

All three of these indicators largely point down into early 2023. The geopolitical cycle turns up slowly in 2020, then the demographic cycle goes down more dramatically from 2023 forward. That's why I am concerned more about the next three years, from early 2020 into early 2023, than about any period we've seen since 1973–75 and 1930–33.

This brings me to the fourth and most recent cycle I've discovered. It's in a more intermediate term and allows us to time cycles beyond the generational spending wave. It came from Ned Davis, who did research on 100 years of the stock market. He found that the worst recessions and stock crashes come in the first two to three years of every decade. He called it the *decennial cycle*. That cycle worked throughout my whole career until 2010–12, when I was predicting a great crash ahead, but it didn't happen. I wondered, "Here's something that worked. It's not working. Is the cycle wrong, or is there something I don't understand?"

I saw an article by a large-fund manager from PIMCO, Paul McCulley, which said that sunspot cycles saved him from the 2000–02 crash. These are not clocklike ten-year cycles; they vary from 8 to 13 years, and that's why it didn't hit in 2010–12.

If we go back to when we start to have good economic data—in the mid-1800s—we find that 88 percent of the substantial recessions, stock crashes, or financial crises occurred in the downside of this cycle. That is an amazingly long-term correlation and cannot be by accident.

People say, "Harry, you can't talk about sunspot cycles; it's too crazy." But these cycles affect the amount of radiation hitting the earth. They affect rainfall. They affect people's moods. Scientists study them because they also affect satellites and electrical infrastructures. The last cycle peaked in February 2014 and looks to bottom between late 2021 and 2022.

Here we have a cycle nobody understands. Ned Davis and people looking for downturns in the early part of the decade were bound to be disappointed when the last cycle hit early in 2008–09, but I have the secret for predicting this. To me, this is the most important cycle because it can be more specific.

I knew that these general cycles were going to peak around 2007, but when should we look for the biggest crashes? All four of these cycles come together from 2020 into 2023. This has not happened since the early to mid-seventies, when we saw the greatest financial crisis and the biggest stock crashes for that generation. Further back, it happened between 1929 and 1934, when we saw the worst of the Great Depression, with an 89 percent stock crash and 25 percent unemployment. It was the worst crisis in modern history, especially for the United States.

Let's step back. The geopolitical cycle started pointing down in late 2001 and does not turn around until about early 2020. The generational spending wave cycle started pointing down from late 2007 and doesn't turn around fully until the latter part of 2023.

The innovation cycle peaked around late 2019, when accounting for its bubble phase, and points down for the longest period—into 2031–32. That cycle is not going to benefit us for a long time.

The next gee-whiz technologies you hear about—whether it be nanotechnologies or robotics or biotech—are going to hit us from 2032 forward, even though they'll hit in a lot of places before that. The sunspot cycle, which is the best for pinpointing crashes and financial crises, points down from 2014 into late 2021–22. So here we are sitting in early 2020, looking forward. This bubble is just getting ready to burst, so it's time to get serious about this. When you put the sunspot cycle together with the others, it says we're going to see the worst financial crisis of our lifetime between mid-2020 and early 2023. Stock cycles most suggest a bottom to the final great crash of this winter season by late 2022.

You need to understand how important this cycle is, because you need to make decisive moves now for your family, your business, and your investments. I joke that if we do not see a major financial crisis between now and early 2023, I am going to quit my profession and become a limo driver in Australia.

There's another dimension to this picture—emerging countries. Emerging countries are becoming an increasingly dominant part of the world economy. This will continue for many decades ahead, because these countries are the only ones that have positive demographic trends (outside of the seven small gainer countries I mentioned earlier). Emerging countries are the future. Almost all developed countries are going to be slowing or declining in the decades ahead.

Emerging countries have the best demographic spending trends in this next boom from 2023 forward, and this is going to last into the 2050s. As I mentioned earlier, China is the exception. China still has the potential to urbanize further, but its demographics will be declining. The boom will happen everybody else. It'll be in the rest of Asia. India will be the star of the next boom. It's going to spread to the Middle East and increasingly to Africa, because these have the youngest populations.

Most emerging countries export commodities to us—everything from energy to industrial and agricultural commodities. When these exports go down, their best industries and stock markets go down, and their best jobs get hurt. The emerging countries have been hit the worst in recent years. Some of them have been down since 2007–08, others since 2011, because commodity prices have been collapsing, and that is their bailiwick. You're probably thinking, "Harry has a cycle for commodities?" Yes, I do. The difference is that this cycle impacts emerging countries when it goes down. Except for the frackers and the energy companies, which are going to get killed by this, the United States in general is glad to see prices go down for oil and other commodities, because in most cases we are commodity buyers, not sellers. It's the emerging world that gets hit.

If I look back in modern history, especially during the last century, I see a 30-year commodity cycle. Commodity prices peak, then they collapse for a decade or a decade and a half, and then they boom again. It reached a peak in 1920. There was a crash in the early 1920s that didn't bottom until the early to mid-thirties, and then we had the next commodity boom. It peaked between 1949 and 1951, went sideways, and crashed a bit. The next bubble—for oil, gold, silver, and commodities in general—peaked in 1980. Then the market crashed, even though we had a general boom.

This commodity cycle is beyond demographic and generational booms and busts. It's its own cycle. If it's crashing when demographic trends are good, it'll go down less. If it's crashing when demographic trends are bad, as is occurring in many countries here ahead, it will be worse.

This 30-year commodity cycle hits emerging countries. They slow. China's slowing hits commodity prices. This is a vicious cycle, and it's now starting to back up on the world, because we, along with Europe and others, also export products to these emerging countries. China is the biggest manufacturing exporter in the world now, and for the first time 51 percent of manufacturing exports are to emerging countries. The epicenter of this next bubble burst that I've been predicting for 2020–22 is going to come from China and the emerging world. It's not going to come from the subprime crisis or weakening demographics in countries like the United States and Japan before. Those things have already been happening. Corporate and government debt defaults in China and the emerging world are likely to be the trigger this time.

Stock markets in emerging countries have already been down 46 percent at worst from their overall peak in 2007–08. They're down 40 percent just since 2011, when commodities peaked and went down for the second time. The

Commodity Research Board (CRB) index, which tracks all commodities grouped together, is down 60 percent from 2008.

Copper, considered the quintessential industrial commodity, is down 75 percent. Oil's been down 80 percent at worst since 2008. This commodity collapse has largely already happened. It's affected emerging countries, but it will hit world trade and economy as well. In a global civilization, you one part of the world impacts everybody. Although commodity prices have rallied in recent years, most will hit new lows into 2021 or 2022 before rebounding with demand from emerging countries that spend more on commodities and will dominate the demographic trends of the next global boom, while most developed countries continue to slow.

Again, commodity prices are killing the emerging world. China is the biggest bubble in history, as I'll show below. This will be the epicenter for the next global bust. Once it happens, it only makes demographic and other cycles get worse.

Chapter Two

Ups and Downs in Real Estate

Almost everybody owns or is involved in real estate in some way or the other. One of the unique things about this bubble is that real estate has been at the center of it.

Look at Japan. Japan had this bubble burst in stocks, real estate, and the general economy way before us, in the early nineties. Since 1997, they've been using quantitative easing as a desperate measure, but all they have is a coma economy, with zero growth and zero inflation on average. It's true that they haven't had a Great Depression like the United States in the thirties, but they're like a patient in the emergency room, living on life support, because they won't let their economy rebalance. They won't let this bubble burst. They're protecting their industries, protecting their government, and protecting the special interests in the banking system. That's not how you do it. Most people are not aware that they have had a boost from their smaller millennial generation into this year, 2020, and their demographic trends will fade even faster in the decades ahead. Hence Japan can print all the money they want and not counter this next round of collapse.

Here I want to focus on real estate, because I recently learned a big lesson from Japan, and I got a huge insight into real estate that I'd never had before.

Japan's real-estate bubble peaked in 1991. That was exactly 42 years after the peak of their baby boom. Japan does everything a year later than the United States. If our peak in real estate was age 41 for the boomers, it was age 42 for them. If our peak in spending was 46, it was 47 for them, so this was right on cue.

In 2005, when I was predicting that the real-estate bubble in the United States would burst, many people told me that was impossible; it couldn't happen. I said, "Have you talked to anybody in Japan?" Japan went down over 60 percent in residential, 80 percent in commercial real estate. Here's the big insight: 24 years later, it still has never bounced back, in either commercial or residential real estate. Their stock market bounced back, and the economy has pulled itself up in recent years with quantitative easing, but real estate hardly bounced hardly at all—even after the next generation came along.

Normally I would lag birth peaks forward 41 or 42 years to find a peak in real estate. Although Japan is a decliner, they did have a substantial younger generation in the late 1990s and early 2000s. They should have been buying real estate, but real estate never bounced back. Why?

After years of banging my head against the wall, I realized that real estate is unique in that it lasts forever. In Europe, typical homes are 300 to 400 years old. There are buildings—castles, churches—that are thousands of years old. This is different from most consumer goods, such as food, clothing, automobiles, or furnishings, which don't last forever. When you have a larger baby-boom generation dying at faster rates than young people are coming along, they cancel them out or more. That's what happened in Japan. By the time their young generation came along and were buying homes, there were as many or more Japanese baby boomers dying, and diers are sellers. In fact a lot of people sell years before they die, because they move into nursing homes or assisted living. This is why Japan didn't get a bounce. It's diers versus buyers.

Hence I came out with a different indicator to account for the different dynamics in real estate. It's like workforce growth, which, as I said earlier, that causes inflation and similar effects, and by the way, commercial real estate. There I have to subtract the retirees at age 63 (on average) from the workforce entrants at age 20 (on average). For real estate I take the peak buyers, age 42 in Japan, 41 in the United States and then I subtract the diers at average life expectancy of 79 in the U.S. or 84 in Japan. People are going to sell and offset those younger buyers. I don't know whether it's the sushi, the seaweed, or the sake, but they're doing something right over there, and I get a whole different thing.

In aging countries, this net demand for houses is going to decline. Germany and Japan are already converting residential and commercial developments into parks, because they don't need the properties. They have to downsize.

When I correlated lagged peak births and death rates in Japan, I got a better correlation with real-estate prices, and I saw why they didn't bounce back. Guess what? They don't ever bounce back; they will even go lower into 2033. Even in the United States, I found that after net demand bounces back up, it turns down until 2039. This doesn't mean housing's going to shrink yet, but the need for new homes will slow down between the late 2020s and the late 2030s. It will actually go negative between 2028 and 2039.

There's going to come a time when we need fewer homes. Home developers don't get this. It's already been the case in the faster-aging countries like Japan and Germany. People in real-estate development have to realize that we're not going to need homes and offices as we did in the past, because the baby-boom generation is dying as fast and in some cases faster than the young generation is coming along.

This is a huge change. This has never happened in history. I wouldn't have figured it out if I hadn't kept studying the Japanese and seeing that their real estate was never the same.

Real estate will never be the same. Remember, most of real estate buying is very concentrated. It's between ages 27 and 41 in the United States, and between ages 28 and 42 in Japan and Europe. (Note that those ages are one year higher for the present millennial generation.) The baby boomers are long over their house-buying boom. No bigger generation is coming that is going to need more houses or cause strong demand. Houses are going to see another downturn. One of my principles, which I'll go into further, is that when bubbles burst, they go back to where they started. We still haven't seen home prices fall back to where they were in early 2000, when the real estate bubble started.

The drop in real-estate prices—34 percent in the United States between 2006 and 2012—was not enough. Real estate is still not affordable for the younger generation. It needs to be. There was a huge bubble in housing, and it needs to come back down to earth. Real estate will never be the same.

I'm predicting another real-estate downturn, starting by early 2021 and possibly sooner. Then there will be a 40 percent plus crash versus 34 percent last time, and it won't bottom until 2025–26, as it took 6 years top to bottom into 2012. We came into the last peak in 2006, 20 percent higher than net demand suggested; this time we are 41 percent higher as of 2019. When bubbles crash, prices are going to go down lower than the fundamentals would suggest, just as they go higher than the fundamentals in the bubble. I think real estate will come back modestly sometime after 2023 and will just grow with inflation in the future—no more bubble real estate!

One great insight came from an economist named Robert Shiller. I picked up on it right away. He and I were the only two people who saw the housing bubble bursting in late 2005, and we were really emphatic about that. Shiller showed that over the long term, housing, unlike stocks, does not grow with the economy; it grows with inflation. When you adjust for inflation, housing doesn't grow over the long term. The same is true for gold, by the way. That's why gold does not do well when we have a downturn that does not have inflation, or when we have a boom without inflation.

Real estate will never be the same. In the future, you will be buying real estate as you did in Monopoly—for the rents or the savings of rents. If you want to own a house, you're going to save the rents you would have paid versus your own mortgage costs, property taxes, and other expenses. You don't buy real estate to get rich anymore, to sit on something and have it go up 10–20 percent a year. That really only happened beyond the normal inflation rate between the beginning of 2000 and the beginning of 2006.

Over six short years, housing went up 130 percent in the United States for no good reason. It went up even more in Japan, even more in other cities and countries around the world. Do you know why? Because banks started lending you nine times your income instead of the traditional amount of three times your income. That's why we had the subprime crisis, and everything went down.

At this point, if you're going to buy real estate for investment, you have to ask, can you rent it out with a positive cash flow many years into the future? You also have to ask, when will consumers or businesses need your property? Again, I can project when workforce growth will rise or fall. In the United States, workforce growth is going to continue to fall into the early 2020s, so I don't want to be buying commercial real estate unless I'm in a really hot area.

If you want to buy foreclosures or other houses on superdeals, below replacement costs, make sure that you can rent them out at positive cash flow for many years in the future, even if rents go down a little. Think like Monopoly. Real estate is a cash-flow stream. You buy it for cash flow, and to save the rents that you would otherwise have paid.

Chapter Three

The China Tsunami

That brings me to my favorite topic at present: the China bubble, which is the greatest one I've seen in all of modern history. It was government-driven. Over the last three decades, the Chinese government moved over 500 million people from rural to urban areas. This always happens when emerging countries are developing. Urbanization is the most important trend for emerging countries, because if you move somebody from a rice paddy even into an unskilled city job—like driving a taxi or working in construction—their income tends to triple. The Chinese figured this out, and they decided to accelerate this process. They're a top-down government. They didn't have to answer to the free markets, investors, voters, or anybody else, and they've created the greatest bubble in history.

At this point, China has so overbuilt housing that 22 percent of houses and condos in major cities are vacant. They're sitting there. They're not bought and then rented out; they're vacant. Nobody's in them.

Affluent Chinese have invested in these properties, and I'll tell you why. The Chinese don't have social safety nets. They also save a lot of money. The average person in China saves 50 percent of his income, versus 2–3 percent in the United States (if we're lucky). The wealthy people, the top 10 percent, who dominate real estate and financial assets just like in the United States, save 70 percent of their income.

Here's the second unique thing about the Chinese: you have to own something, Unless a man owns real estate, he doesn't have any chance for getting married or even getting a date. So even though their incomes are a tenth of those in the United States, the Chinese have 92 percent real-estate ownership. Ours in the United States is 62 percent, down from 67 percent at the top, which is more typical for the world.

The third thing that is unique in China is that in the United States, the typical family will have maybe a third, and after the downturn, 27 percent, of their net worth in real estate. The rest is in stocks, bonds, and savings accounts. Not the Chinese. They have 75 percent of their financial assets and net worth in real estate.

The Chinese save a lot, and they love real estate. Everybody has to own something. They also speculate, with high percentages of second and third homes bought. Their biggest long-term investment is real estate, and they'll buy it empty. They think real estate always goes up, because that's all they've seen. You have to remember that just four decades ago, in the Mao era, home ownership was for the most part simply not allowed largely. So they really are naive in this arena.

Property values in Shanghai have gone up 860 percent since the early 2000s, and that's not as bad as in Beijing. (For comparison, U.S. real estate went up 130 percent before the last bubble burst and then went down.) This is the greatest bubble in any major country in the world. My projection is that Shanghai's bubble could crash 78 percent, more than Japan's bubble did, and far more than that of the U.S.

Furthermore, the government supports real-estate investment. The local communist parties receive guaranteed loans or support for getting loans easily from the state-owned banks. Shadow banks take money from wealthy people that can't get any yield, so the banks fund these projects. They even built several cities. One of them is Ordos City in Inner Mongolia. It's built for a million people, but there's almost nobody in it. It has the largest mall in the world, but they built in the middle of the country, where you need it least. Since they couldn't get any stores or businesses in there, they've turned it into a theme park, like a Disney World, to attract tourism.

The Chinese are overbuilding everything. They have bridges, roads, railways to nowhere—beyond anything we could imagine. They used more cement in one decade than the United States used in 100 years of building.

This is crazy, but the worst thing is that the affluent Chinese, who own some 70 percent of the personal real estate and some 80 percent of investment real estate, buy these properties and let them sit. They don't even rent them out. They're expecting to flip them down the road. They have massive amounts of the nation's net worth invested this way, and they think the government won't let it go down. A large audience in Dubai told me that, just before their sudden 40 percent crash in 2007.

People love to speculate. They love bubbles. It's something for nothing. Bubbles don't last, because they aren't real. They go up too fast, and everybody jumps in, because everybody wants to get rich quick and go to heaven financially, but everybody can't do that. Somebody has to work and do something real.

China's been moving 500 million people into cities. The government is having them build things in order to create jobs. The idea is that they're such a large country and still have more rural people to move into cities in future decades, so one day they'll need these properties. But what happens if the bubble bursts in between, and all this wealth evaporates, as it did for the Japanese in the early nineties? This is worse. China's has been much more pervasive.

The Chinese love to move to English-speaking cities for their kids, and these are the cities bubbling the most outside of China: Singapore, Sidney, Melbourne, and Brisbane are the biggest beneficiaries. It's also the whole West Coast in the United States: San Diego, Los Angeles, San Francisco, Seattle, as well as Toronto, New York, and London. The Chinese love to move to these places and buy real estate, and they buy in cash.

Let me explain why they're doing this. Rich Chinese are richer relative to their economy than even the rich people here, and they have been getting richer faster than any time in their modern history. That's not going to last, and it's feeding the bubble, because rich people invest the most in financial assets and real estate. When they run out of money or they go bust, the rich get hurt the most.

Here's what unique about the Chinese. The Chinese government is telling people there, "We don't want you taking your capital out of the country. You can only move $50,000 a year legally." On the other hand, the government isn't going to tell a Chinese person who moves for four years for their kids to go to college in Southern California or New York or London that they can't buy a house while they're there. They're not going to tell a Chinese businessperson who invests in a business in America or Australia or England that they can't invest in real estate for their business.

When the rich Chinese get around this restriction on capital, they're essentially laundering their money. That's why they buy the most expensive real estate they can find, and they pay all cash. They want to get as much money out. They don't trust their government. They know it's a top-down bureaucracy, and one day the communist government is going to turn against the most productive people. The richest Chinese are planning to leave or already have left the country. They're doing it under the guise of their kids' education or business overseas. When the China bubble bursts—and it's already starting—they're going to say sayonara: "I'm out of here; come get me if you want."

The Chinese have as many of their assets as possible overseas, where the Chinese government cannot get to it. This is unique—much bigger than what the Japanese did. Again, real estate is slowing around the world. There are more and more developed countries, more diers than buyers, slowing trends and buying after the baby boom has long matured.

Other people—the Brazilians and Latin Americans—are buying real estate in the United States, especially in places like Miami because that's where they can find their ethnic communities. They're getting money out of their country. They don't trust their governments. Their economies are already crumbling. Drug dealers love to walk into Miami and buy condos with a bag of cash, like Bugsy Siegel in the Great Depression.

Everybody in Vancouver, San Francisco, Sidney, and London thinks their bubble can't go down. Why? Because of the foreign buyers: they think everybody wants to live there. But these foreign buyers don't live there; they're laundering money. They may be there part-time or temporarily for their kids, but they have real estate back home (if they haven't left their countries). They're going to have to sell your real estate to protect theirs, which is exactly what the Japanese did.

I call it the China tsunami. They've built a bubble that's not sustainable. There's no way these 500 million people can keep having jobs and building buildings when everything's empty already—factories, roadways, infrastructure, offices, malls, homes, and condos. You can't sustain that trend, and when this bubble bursts, these people are going to be trapped.

Now I'll give you another interesting statistic. Out of these 500 million that have moved from rural to urban areas, presently 221 million—and these are the people that have moved in the last twelve years—are not even legal citizens in the cities they live in. They're like illegal immigrants in the United States. They move to the cities, but they never qualify for citizenship there, because these cities don't want to give instant citizenship to everybody that moves in, only to the people that have been there for a while. These rural immigrants are illegal citizens. They don't have access to health care. They don't have access to education for their kids. They will not get the few welfare benefits the government provides.

When times are good, nobody cares; it kind of works and people get by. But when this game of musical chairs stops in China, you're going to have 220 million people trapped in these cities.

Many of them can't even go back to where they are citizens and get some benefits. They can't go back to their rice paddies, because these have been paved over to make room for empty condos. Local governments buy the land, put up condos for nobody, and the local people move into the city.

This is going to be the biggest bubble burst in modern history. Everybody's saying that the Chinese government has control of the economy, so they can have a soft landing. But mark my words: China's going to fall like an elephant, and when it does, it's going to send shock waves around the world, because it's now the second-largest economy in the world, having passed Japan many years ago. China says it's growing at a rate 7 percent a year. But local people and forecasters I know say it's 3–4 percent max, and it's going to be negative soon.

China's going to slow world growth. It will kill emerging countries even more, because it will kill commodities. It's also going to cause the strongest real-estate bubbles to burst, especially in the leading English-speaking cities, where the Chinese like to send their kids to college and launder money outside of their country.

China's stock-market bubble is still down 50 percent from its 2007 top after a 70 percent crash in one year in 2008, and in the next year and a half, I think it's going to be down 80 percent plus. Real estate's going to follow, and it's going to be down 70 percent or more in many cities.

Chapter Four

Bubble Wealth

There is another important thing to understand about what's happening. Globally, when stocks go down, they all go down; some just go down faster and to different degrees.

Real estate's more like popcorn. The Japan bubble burst first, and everybody thought it was an anomaly. Then it burst in the United States, Spain, and then Ireland. People were still saying, "Those are anomalies. Our bubbles won't burst."

But it's like a popcorn popper. The more kernels burst, the faster the process accelerates.

In some leading cities, like London, New York, San Francisco, and Vancouver, the bubbles are insane. The last time I was in Vancouver, my taxi driver was living in a $1.1 million shack. I told him, "This is a glorified trailer. You should sell that thing while you can. This is crazy."

When everyday people can't afford to live in a place anymore, they start to riot. People in Vancouver are starting to protest. People in Singapore have already forced the government there to keep the Chinese from buying in order to stop speculation and penalize foreign buyers. As a result, real estate in Singapore is falling the fastest in Asia. San Francisco residents have been protesting foreign buyers, especially buyers from Silicon Valley. They hate Google, because executives come from around the world. These companies force up real-estate speculation, so everyday people have to move out of the city.

This is going to end. Not only is the China tsunami going to wreck the global economy, it's going to set off a broader pop in real estate. None of these real-estate markets are ever going to be the same. Look for real estate to burst around the world at least as much as it burst back in 2006–12 in countries like the United States.

The hardest things to argue with people about are gold and real estate. I can talk people out of owning stocks and commodities, but people are personally attached to their real estate and to owning real estate in the first place.

We've been in a unique period of history since World War II, when, as I said earlier, the first middle-class generation could broadly afford homes. That caused an unbelievable boom in home buying from the fifties forward. Most baby boomers have lived in a time when real estate did nothing but go up, and we're convinced it can never go down. That is the worst assumption you can make.

As I said before, during the last bubble, in 2000–06, banks went from loaning on a mortgage from three times your income to nine times, and incomes didn't even go up that much. That's what fueled the bubble. In addition to strong demand and demographics, it takes debt to fuel a bubble.

We have seen the greatest debt bubble in modern history. This occurs periodically, but only once in a lifetime, so nobody's around to remember the last one. Our last great debt bubble occurred from 1914 into 1929—the Roaring Twenties. After causing a minor bubble in real estate and a big bubble in stocks, it crashed, and we had the Great Depression. We had to write off a lot of debt. That takes money out of the economy that had been created as if by magic and then disappears.

Bubble wealth, which people thought they had in stocks or real estate, then disappears and doesn't come back for a long time. When bubbles burst, you get deflation. Here's the key insight, and you have to get this even if you have to read it many times: when bubbles burst in debt and in financial assets, *money disappears*.

This money was created solely by debt. When banks make loans, they don't pull the money out of their pockets. They can lend ten times a reserve of 10 percent of deposits—and that's *your* money; it's not even theirs. They're also supposed to have capital and other reserves to back up their loans, but even that amounts only to a small percentage.

Banks are creating money out of nothing. It's called the *fractional reserve system*. This was only created back in the early 1900s, when the Federal Reserve was created. It's another reason we've had larger stock and real-estate bubbles ever since the Fed was created, outside of the monumental Midwest immigration bubble that peaked in the 1830s from heavy government incentives and low-cost finance. The Fed's approach is to always push down interest rates to stimulate the economy. They have refused to let bubbles rebalance, so they've created a system whereby banks can lend at a rate ten to one of their reserves. They're creating money out of thin air.

The other way we create money is through quantitative easing. Central banks print money and throw it into the system to keep stimulating the economy, but this only creates bubbles. Unlike normal stimulus to encourage bank lending, this new program put the money directly into financial assets as central banks buy bonds and other assets with money printed out of thin air. That means more money chasing the same stocks, bonds, and real estate, and driving them ever up. That creates financial asset inflation instead of consumer price inflation. As consumers and businesses, we'd already borrowed too much money in the Great Boom from 1983 to 2007; hence normal stimulus for bank lending didn't work to cure the great recession of 2008.

Governments have run deficits in both good and bad times. They're only supposed to run them in bad times. Many countries have run budget deficits in since the early seventies, so we've had the greatest debt bubble in history.

In the megaboom from 1983 to 2008, there was four times as much private debt as government debt. Total debt in the U.S. grew 2.6 times GDP in the 26 years from 1983 through 2008. How could economists not see a problem with that? When something finally goes wrong, you have a debt deleveraging, and you have a depression.

I'll give you the global picture. Total debt in the global economy is now over $250 trillion. This is money that can actually disappear, because it consists of loans, stocks, and bonds. This figure doesn't count real estate, but even real estate is largely backed by mortgages.

From looking at the Great Depression, when a lot of debt was written off and financial assets burst, I'm saying that a minimum of $100 trillion could disappear from the global economy in the next several years. When you have less money in the economy chasing financial assets and consumer goods, you get deflation in prices. This is important.

At this point practically nobody has seen deflation in their lifetime, except briefly in late 2008 and early 2009 in a few pockets here and there. We did see deflation in financial-asset prices, and a lot of debt was written off. This was a good thing in the long term.

How is the young generation today going to invest when stocks are so overvalued that the best models say you'd be lucky to get –1 to –3 percent over the next decade? How can you afford to buy a home when prices are much higher, adjusted for inflation, than at any time in modern history? High real-estate costs are only good for investors or businesses that already own it. They're terrible for young generations coming along, and the young generation is the future. This is a reason that we're going to see deflation despite massive money printing. The goldbugs have it dead wrong here. For years I've been making bets with these guys. I've been saying that gold will go lower and lower, and it has.

In late April 2011, in our free newsletter, we told people to sell gold and silver right at the $49 peak, which was at an all-time high since 1980. Several months later, gold went down after going only 5 or 6 percent higher. We got people out at the right time, because the bubble seemed to be peaking and the commodity cycle was peaking. Goldbugs claimed that because we were printing money, we were going to have inflation. It was supposedly going to turn into hyperinflation, because the government was going to print more and more. Although gold and silver have bounced into early 2020, I still see gold bottoming, best case, at a slight new low, around $1,000, or more likely back to the 2008 lows near $700. Silver could bottom between $6 and $8.

But there are limits. The U.S. has already stopped printing money. Japan can barely grow, even though it's doing three times the money printing we've ever done. Europe is printing strongly again, but they can barely grow. There's a limit to what you can do this way. At some point, something goes wrong, like the China tsunami or a crash in oil prices. No government's going to buy oil to prop prices up; they can't. The U.S. and European central banks can't stop the China bubble from bursting, because China's not printing money so much as overbuilding; it's a completely different thing.

I've been looking for some global factors that might trigger the next bubble burst, just as the subprime crisis did in the United States in 2008. That crisis didn't take place everywhere; it happened in four states: California, Arizona, Nevada, and Florida. They had the biggest bubbles and the biggest subprime crisis. When those loans went bad and junk bonds went bad, borrowing for risky enterprises went up. Then everybody started looking out for risk, and we had a global crisis. In fact, we had a global crisis, because demographics in most countries were slowing. Even though debt levels were much higher than in the Roaring Twenties or in any previous bubble, it took a trigger to start it. As I mentioned earlier, that could be corporate and government debt defaults in the emerging world, where most of the new debt has come since the 2008 financial crisis. That's just the beginning.

Every way I look at it, this, the greatest debt bubble in history, will make the Roaring Twenties bubble look like nothing. The stock market is not likely to exceed the 89 percent crash into 1932, but this bubble has occurred in all financial assets and much more globally. Real estate will definitely see a larger crash than the 1930s. Of course debt bubbles are bigger today, because as we get wealthier, we can borrow more. Central banks around the world want the economy to look better today, so they tend to keep interest rates too low, making borrowing too easy. When things go wrong, they print a lot of money and try to cure the debt crisis with more debt. It's not going to happen.

We're going to see more debt deleveraging than you will see in an entire lifetime—possibly until your kids or grandkids will see—in the next great bubble that'll burst in the 2070s. (I'm just saying that to show you how far we can predict ahead with demographics in our key cycles. You can see the future over the rest of your lifetime.)

Chapter Five

Ten Signs of Bursting Bubbles

L et me discuss what I call the ten principles of bubbles. As I said earlier, I have studied bubbles throughout modern history. The first famous one was the Dutch tulip bubble in 1637. This was the first time people could buy agricultural futures, and the rich started speculating in them. We had the first major bubble in modern history before there was even a stock market. Prices went up exponentially for two years, burst, and went all the way back to where they started.

When it comes to bubbles, people are idiots. We're the smartest species on earth, the most innovative; we're taking over the world to an almost dangerous degree, destroying all other species, because we are so intelligent. But we are deaf, dumb, and blind when it comes to bubbles. They're like a drug. It makes you feel good. You're getting something for nothing. Once you are addicted, either to drugs or to credit or bubbles, you come down, like a drug addict on detox. It's very painful. That's why the depressions that come once in a lifetime, like those in the 1830s and '40s or the 1930s, are the worst times in history, especially when real estate is a big part of tit.

Let me give you a quick list of some of the key bubbles.

- The tulip bubble peaked in 1637 and rapidly burst.

- The South Seas Bubble in England and the Mississippi Bubble in France both peaked in 1720. They burst faster and harder than any other bubble we've seen in modern history, because this was the first time that stock speculation occurred. When people do something the first time, they're naive about it.

- The depression of 1837–43. We had the Great Canal and Midwest real-estate bubble, because the U.S. government was trying to get people to move into the Midwest. They were giving away land supercheap and financing it at superlow interest rates. That's how you create a bubble. When real estate bursts, it makes deleveraging even worse.

- Next was the railroad bubble. This took place around the time the transcontinental railroads were being built. It burst in 1873, beginning a five-year depression when railroad stocks unwound, but because it wasn't a real-estate oriented bubble as such, it didn't have the impact of the previous one.

- The Roaring Twenties bubble burst in 1929. People usually say that was a stock bubble, and that's the most obvious part. At the end, 40 percent of bank loans were made to investors as margin loans on stocks. How can that end well? But that was not the big thing.

The Roaring Twenties bubble wasn't just about auto stocks and other new growth industries; it was a tractor bubble. U.S. agriculture had a kick start in the previous decade from feeding Europe during World War I. We kept expanding afterwards, because tractors were being introduced, which made farms much more profitable. Banks were doing most of their lending for farms and farm equipment. Then the farms went under, and that's what made that so powerful a depression. When the Roaring Twenties turned into the Great Depression, the banks that failed were smaller regional banks in rural areas. It was these banks, not the bigger ones, that went under. It was a farm bust.

After the gold, oil, and commodities bubble in 1980, we saw the tech bubble. That was stock speculation. When that burst between 2000 and 2002, we had a very minor recession in 2001. Again, it wasn't a real-estate bubble. The real-estate bubble started in 2000. That peaked in late 2005–early 2006. Then we had the great financial crisis, because the subprime crisis generated a real-estate bust.

The coming one is the worst. Since 2008, we haven't had demographic trends in our favor. It's just artificial stimulus going into Wall Street and financial institutions. It's not being lent and spent, because we've already had peak debt. Consumers have already borrowed more than they can handle, and businesses are borrowing to buy back their own stock. Governments are buying back their own bonds—that's cheating. If companies buy back their own stock with cheap money, their earnings per share go up, and the executives get stock options for doing nothing. This is bad stuff. After the nineties, our economies switched from productive investment to unproductive speculation, and that's when you're going to see a great depression to follow.

Here are the nine principles of bubbles. They're true of basically every major bubble in history, some more than others.

1. All growth is exponential, not linear. If you have returns at 3 percent a year and reinvest the income, your growth is exponential. Exponential growth always leads to a bubble at some point.

2. All growth is cyclical, not incremental. Over the long term, growth is exponential, but even

exponential growth comes in surges and busts. Whenever you have an extreme bubble, you're going to have an extreme crash.

3. Bubbles always burst. When a bubble is at its top, everybody thinks that we're in a permanent period of prosperity and that this time it won't burst, but it always does. There are no exceptions.

   I love to give this example: If you drop grains of sands continuously onto the floor, it'll build a mound of sand, and it'll get steeper and steeper, in the shape of a Hershey's kiss. Eventually you will have an avalanche, but it will be only one grain of sand that does it. It's hard to know which grain of sand will make it happen, but you know that avalanche is coming.

4. The greater the bubble, the greater the burst. The businesses or the stocks that are the hottest think, "We're the ones that can't burst." I don't care if you're Apple. I don't care if you have the most expensive condo in downtown Manhattan: if you've bubbled up the most, you're going to burst the most when things finally come down.

5. This is very important, because it allows me to make projections most people wouldn't be able to make: bubbles tend to go back to where they started or a bit lower. This is true in nine out of ten cases, and when it's not, it's close. The 1929 bubble, when it burst, went a good bit below where it started in the early twenties. U.S. real estate has not yet come back even to the levels of January 2000, when the market started to grow exponentially. This principle enables me to say that stocks are likely to go at least as low as before; if things are worse, they'll go a little lower.

6. Financial bubbles tend to become more extreme over time, because as income and wealth expand, more credit is available to fuel them.

7. Bubbles become so attractive that they eventually suck in even the skeptics. In the South Seas bubble of the early 1700s, one of the most extreme in history, Sir Isaac Newton came out in public and said, "I'm a scientist, I'm a rational guy, and this is crazy." But it kept going up and up, and finally at the end

guess who jumped in? Sir Isaac Newton, and he got creamed.

8. No one wants the high of easy gains to end. You're getting something for nothing, so you go into denial as the bubble develops, especially in its later stages. When I first moved to Miami in 2005–06, I had seen a bubble developing in California. My wife knew everybody in Miami. We told at least 100 couples that the bubble was going to burst. Not one person sold a thing, and most of them are in trouble now.

9. Major bubbles occur only once in a human lifetime. The last one was the Roaring Twenties and the Great Depression. So it's very hard for the present generation to understand bubbles, how they burst, and why you get deflation and a depression. They've never seen one—baby boomers especially. Because we boomers have been such an inflationary force in the economy, we've only seen inflation for our whole lives. We've never seen deflation. We've never seen a major bubble burst, except in other countries, like Japan.

But we are going to see it happen in the next four to five years.

It's time now to cash out of every bubble you're involved in. Do it now. Don't wait to see, because the first crash tends to be fastest and the most severe—typically 30 percent to 50 percent.

Within two and a half months of the 1929 crash, the Dow was down 49 percent. (Eventually it was down 89 percent, but that took almost three years.) If you waited, it was already too late. You'd already seen most of the crash. In the first two and a half months of the tech wreck in early and mid-2000, the market was down 40 percent. In the end it went down 78 percent, but much of the damage took place in the first two months.

Extreme bubbles don't correct; they burst. And they don't burst 30–60 percent in stocks, like most major bull markets; they typically burst 70–90 percent. This is not something to sit through; you can't use a buy-hold strategy. You can't listen to your stockbroker who says, "You're diversified; stocks always come back." Let me tell you what happened in the 1929 bubble. If you had bought stocks at the top of the market in 1929, they would have crashed 89 percent by July 1932. It took till 1953—twenty-four years— to get back to those levels. It's been the same in every bubble since. Don't sit through bubbles.

Take off the rose-colored glasses. We are in the greatest bubble in modern history. The worst of it is not in the United States or Europe; it is in China, and the China tsunami is going to bring down the entire globe. It's already happening with its slowing of growth and the trade war. Get out of these bubbles now.

Chapter Six

The Four Seasons of an Economy

Now let me give you my most comprehensive model for forecasting the economy, which blends all of the key indicators that I've developed over 30 years.

Everything moves in four stages, with seasons or life cycles. This is a universal principle. In weather, we have spring, summer, fall, and winter. In life we have youth, early adulthood, midlife, and retirement.

Combining all my cycles, I've come up with a four-season model. You have a spring boom, when we come out of a depression, and we have a new generation and a rising economy. After deflation and the deleveraging of the economy, inflation only grows slowly. That's a great economy. That's like our economy in the United States from 1942 to 1968: a boom with modest inflation.

When the next generation comes along and is larger, you get inflation. As I've said, when the baby boom entered the workforce into the late seventies, inflation skyrocketed, while the Bob Hope generation's spending wave declined. From late 1968 to late 1982, we had worse and worse recessions and higher and higher unemployment and higher and higher inflation. Economists called it *stagflation*—inflation combined with recession—but they had no clue what was causing it. Everybody blamed it on the government and government deficits. The government didn't cause it. Government deficits came from the higher cost of inflation and the bad economy.

This is the summer inflation season. In the 1970s, we saw high inflation. It's like the weather when it's hot and muggy. It was like slugging through mud. But it wasn't like the Depression; everything wasn't freezing over.

This is followed by the fall boom. The next generation, in this case the baby boom, enters the workforce. They're getting more productive; they're spending more money. The economy is booming; the new generation is bringing in more powerful technologies, such as personal computers, the Internet, cell phones, and broadband.

This fall season, I call it, sees falling inflation, as (in this case) the baby boomers become productive. The most powerful killer apps of the new technology cycles come in. It's the strongest boom, coming from the largest generation. Historically, this is when immigration flourishes. Immigration flourished into the Roaring Twenties, and then it dropped in the thirties. It didn't flourish in the fifties and sixties boom, but it flourished again in the 1980s, 1990s, and 2000s.

These things come together to create a fall boom—rapidly falling inflation, which makes everything less expensive, including mortgages and car loans. It makes stocks worth more, because lower inflation means lower interest rates to compete with bonds. Higher earnings from lower borrowing costs—everything conspires to create a bubble boom. The last bubble boom was from 1914 to 1929. This most recent one was 1983 to 2007. It was more extreme as a result of low interest rates courtesy of the Federal Reserve.

What follows the bubble boom? Of course—a bubble burst. It's the winter season. When bubbles burst, debt is restructured, money that had been created out of nothing disappears, and financial assets that had been going up for decades crash and stay in the doldrums for at least a decade. Money and wealth disappear, causing deflation.

In the winter season—a falling economy with deflation—everything freezes over. It's the most difficult, challenging economy, and it shifts market share to the strongest businesses, who benefit unbelievably. It creates huge bargains and financial assets for the few investors that were smart enough to get out of the bubble, like Joseph P. Kennedy.

These are the four seasons of our economy. They're projectable. I've been predicting these seasons all the way back to late 1980s, when I was predicting the fall boom and how strong it would be. If you understand these seasons, you can project, not just economic trends in general, but inflation, disinflation, and deflation, as well as when new technologies will emerge into the mainstream.

As an individual or a business, you have to have a different strategy for each season. Too many business consultants and financial advisors have an all-weather strategy: here's what good businesses do to succeed; here's how investors diversify and have asset allocation. It doesn't work that way.

Asset allocation works in most seasons. It does *not* work in the winter season. It's so challenging for businesses that most of them go under, are restructured, or consolidate dramatically. Only a small percentage of businesses are going to emerge from the winter season into spring. That's exactly what the economy wants. It's in the bubble boom that the most important technologies for decades to come.

In the bubble boom, the most important technologies for decades to come emerge, and with cheap credit and low interest rates, a lot of entrepreneurs get easy financing, just as they did in the tech bubble of the nineties. Anybody with a business plan could get money; you didn't even have to have sales or earnings. You could borrow money at low rates. After the tech wreck and especially after the great financial crisis, that was over.

So you let a thousand flowers bloom, and then you shake down to the 5 or 10 percent of companies that have really innovated. Venture capitalists understand that. Even when they have the best ventures coming in, they know they're going to make almost all their money on one out of eleven. That's the real nature of innovation, especially radical innovations. Economists don't understand this whatsoever. I do, because I've worked with new ventures. I started my own business. I've invested in new ventures. I'm only going to make it on one or two out of fifteen. It's brutal, but that's what's happens.

The winter season clears the deck—the excess debt, the speculation, the bubbles, the businesses that didn't do the right thing or see the season shifting. It clears them out so we can move into the spring season again and start a whole new 80-year cycle. Yes, this four-season model occurs over a human lifetime. It used to be 50 to 60 years. They used to call it the Kondratiev wave. They didn't know what drove it.

Now I do. I can time this four-season model with demographic and other indicators. This is a huge breakthrough, and it's something you need to understand. It's saying that despite endless government stimulus, we're going to go into the winter season anyway, because we put it off, creating even bigger bubbles and more debt around the world. It's going to be even worse than it would have been if it had hit more fully from 2008–09 forward. Get ready for the great winter season.

Chapter Seven

Strategies for the Winter Season

I'm going to show the signs that this bubble is bursting, and I'll talk about what to do in your life, your business, and your investments at this point.

As I write this in January 2020, we're finally seeing clear signs that the bubble is bursting. Governments have been fighting this for years and year, with Trump adding corporate tax cuts and deregulation to the efforts on the fiscal side. Next is likely to come a payroll tax holiday or checks in the mail (helicopter money) to consumers when the economy continues to weaken ahead.

But the number-one thing I've seen, the first sign, was a series of key stock market tops around the world, after the Trump bump from late 2016, in early January of 2018. I got more bullish again when Trump won against the odds and the Dow had a 3,000-point overnight reversal. I finally declared we were entering the orgasmic final blow-off phase or the bubble. That top looked like a blow-off top at first. But by early February I could tell that it wasn't.

My analysis of the last 7 major stock bubbles in the last century shows that the first crash averages 42 percent in the first 2.6 months—ranging from 30 percent to 49 percent. The most extreme was that 49 percent in the Dow in 1929 in 2.3 months—the very crash on a 90-year superbubble cycle that I compare to this one. The least was the 30 percent crash in Japan, because their bubble burst alone in a more bullish period for the global economy. That January crash was limited to 10 percent and did not follow that 42 percent crash scenario.

What has happened since? Stocks keep moving more sideways, making slight new highs. But each correction thus far has been deeper. The second correction was 25 percent in late 2018. This is potentially shaping up to be a classic megaphone pattern; if that is the case, we are in the final up wave. This wave has broken higher than the past one, in what is called an *overthrown pattern*, which would signal a top. January started out with the assassination of Iran's top general in a drone strike, and stocks pulled back at first. If they break below 26,300 on the Dow, we should see a fallback of up to 33 percent, from its 28,873 top to around 19,500. Then Trump would easily argue for a full-out Fed monetary stimulus and a direct fiscal stimulus to consumers. We would get a final steep rally, where I would predict that the leading tech stocks in the NASDAQ would make a new high, but the broader indices, like the Dow and S&P 500, wouldn't. Then that would signal a top and I would then expect that 42+ percent crash.

If this is the scenario, you should not wait for that to happen. You should get out of stocks and hedge through strategies, like cheap put options, in such a strong top.

This megaphone pattern is something I've been talking about for years, as there is a giant one forming over a larger time frame. It's so obvious that any stock analyst can see it, but they're in denial; they don't want to. They don't see it, because it only tends to occur rarely in major topping patterns. The last time stocks peaked at the end of a generation's spending cycle was between the mid-sixties and the early seventies, We had a series of higher highs. There was a high late in 1965; then it crashed. Then there was a slightly higher high late in 1968, then a deeper crash. The last high was late in 1972, and the deepest crash in that whole series happened into late 1974. That crash was 50 percent, right down to where the trendline through the progressively lower bottoms projected. How do you draw this megaphone pattern? There was already a series of slightly higher highs and progressively lower lows. You draw a trend line through the tops and the bottoms, and it looks like a it looks like a megaphone. You can project where the thing is likely to end by where the final correction hits the bottom trend line.

We've seen a similar pattern, with a much larger topping pattern, since early 2000. We had the bubble that peaked in March 2000. We had the tech wreck into late 2002 with the Dow down

46 percent and the much bubblier NASDAQ down 78 percent. We had the second bubble into late 2007 to marginally higher highs; then that crashed, and it went to lower lows, down 54 percent. The third and final wave was exaggerated by the massive and unprecedented QE injection of $17 trillion over 10 years, rising into the financial markets and creating the biggest and largest bubble in history during the weakest recovery in history. That's called an *overthrow peak* and is a sign of the final top. As of early January 2020, we are still in this larger overthrow final wave pattern and in a potential peak in the shorter 2-year megaphone pattern.

What do you do? If you want to be like Joseph Kennedy in late 1929, what do you do right now to prepare your life, your business, and your investments?

I'm going to start with investing, because it's the most straightforward. In the winter season, the choices are very narrow. Everything goes down. People who are involved in investments remember the 2008–09 crash. Gold and silver went down in the latter part. Commodities went down. Real estate went down. Stocks, emerging markets, Europe, the United States, around the world, China—everything went down, even in Australia, although they didn't have a recession.

The only thing that went up was the U.S. dollar versus other currencies, and the highest-quality longer-term bonds, especially those denominated in U.S. currency. We are the reserve currency, and we created the most debt in U.S. dollars, so we see that the most debt destroyed the most debt. That makes the dollar more valuable. During these periods, the currency in which you destroy the most debt is the one that is worth most. Eventually, that could be China, but their massive overbuilding and debt bubble will take the longest to sort out. When there's less of something, it's worth more. Most people don't get that.

In the second half of 2008, when the financial crisis was at its worst, the dollar went up 27 percent. Everything else went down more like 50 percent, or more typically, except for real estate, 34 percent. Gold was down 33 percent, silver 50 percent. There was nowhere to hide.

That's what you have to do again this time again. It's just going to be bigger. We have a bigger bubble: we have more extremes, more debt, more deleveraging, more to crash, so you have to look for safe assets. In other words, your goal here is to preserve your wealth. Cash out of the bubble. Don't go searching for higher yields.

For many years now, all this quantitative easing has told you that you can hardly make any money on a short-term T-bill or money-market fund and you can only get 2 percent at best on a 10-year Treasury bond. When you adjust for inflation, that's zero. You're getting zero. That's not good. And many bonds are giving negative real interest in Europe and Japan. How do you save for retirement? You don't.

Don't do what most people are doing, saying, "Since I can only get 2 percent on a government bond, I'd better go into a corporate bond or a junk bond that pays higher interest rates, 3, 4, 5, 6 percent." Don't do that. Those bonds are going to get hit by defaults in a worsening economy, and the higher the yield, the more the bond's going go down. In the last crash in 2008, junk bonds went down as yields went up and risk went up with default. They went down as much as stocks did—50 percent in general. So you don't want to be in junk bonds. Even corporate bonds rated below AAA go down some with a bad economy. You want to be in the highest-quality Treasury bonds. Shorter-term bonds better at first; as we get into this crisis, you may go for longer-term bonds, where you may be able to lock in slightly higher yields.

Get into safe, cashlike T-bills if you want to be totally safe. If you want some yield to replace your dividends from stocks, get a 2 percent–plus 10-year Treasury or a 2.5 percent–plus 30-year Treasury bond over this crisis. They will do well, even though yields will jump up and down at times when people get scared.

In the 1930s, the only major sector of investments that made money were the highest-quality AAA corporate bonds and Treasury bonds. They pretty much doubled during the thirties, when stocks totally crashed and never came close to recovering. Real estate totally crashed and came back by the end of the decade, but commodities and everything else went down.

There is a huge benefit to simply being in safe assets or cashlike assets; let everything fall and then reinvest. That's what Joseph Kennedy did, as I said earlier: he sold his stocks. He took all of his money out of his investments, cashed it out, and then bought legitimate businesses in the downturn. You use your cash built up from cashing out of the bubble to reinvest in all types of financial assets, including stocks, real estate, and businesses. When things are down, people need cash. Cash and cash flow are the secret to the winter season.

If you have real estate that you can rent out at positive cash flow now (and even if rents go down a certain amount), you can keep that. Rentals are in a positive demographic cycle that is peaking around 2018–19 but should extend into a downturn where rentals are favored over buying homes. When it gets harder for families and businesses to borrow to buy real estate, more people want to rent, both commercially and residentially.

How do you benefit from the rise in the dollar? I see world currency as very simple. The U.S. dollar has been down in the boom; it's lower in value than in 1985. All other currencies have gone up, but when we go into this great reset and deleveraging, like in 2008, the U.S. dollar's going to go up, and most other currencies are going to go down. But as occurred last time, this may come several months into the crisis, likely more in 2021–22. There are indexes that measure the U.S. dollar versus the currencies of our six major trading partners. It's called the *dollar index*. There is an ETF, an electronically traded fund, called the UUP, which you can buy just like a stock and which largely tracks the U.S. dollar versus other currencies. If you had bought the UUP in early 2008 when this crisis was starting, you would have been up 27 percent at the worst. You would have made money in an investment that's been up 38 percent since early 2008 and never gone to new lows since.

Even in the recovery, the U.S. dollar, even though it's gone down at times, has never gone to as low as the beginning of the crisis. Here in early 2020, the US dollar is still up 36 percent. This has been a great safe haven and may be due to some downside volatility in 2020. I'm predicting that as the next crisis gets worse into 2021–22, the dollar will go up another 20–25 percent from here, but it may correct a bit first into 2020. That would be the time to buy. You can only get this in a bullish dollar fund, and there are plenty of those, if you talk to a stock broker or a financial advisor, or buy the UUP.

You have your cash, safe assets, and cash-flow-generating assets; you have part of your portfolio you can put into dollars. The only other thing you can really do is to take a part of your portfolio and realize that stocks have been going up forever. They're so overvalued that, according to the models, you're lucky to make -3 percent over the next decade. That's not good.

So first of all, get out of stocks over the next decade. You're not going to miss anything, even if I'm a little wrong about how this works out or when. You don't do this full-out. You can take a part of your portfolio, depending on your risk tolerance—it might be 10 or 20 percent—and bet on stocks going down. You can buy an ETF, which is easy to buy and sell, that goes inverse to the index.

If you want to bet that the S&P 500, the broadest stock market in the U.S., will go up, you buy something like an ETF called SPY, which tracks the S&P 500. If you want to bet that it will go down, you buy SH, an inverse fund. If the S&P 500 does go down 60–70 percent into mid- to late-2022, you're going to make roughly 60–70 percent. Don't do that with all of your portfolio, because this can be very volatile, but decide how much you want to bet on a decline in the stock market.

Just as you use risk tolerance and diversification on the way up, you use them on the way down. The difference is that in the latter case, your choices are much narrower. Buy safe, high-quality AAA corporate bonds and U.S. Treasury bonds, short-term at first, building to longer-term if yields go up at times, and then watch those yields go down. Your bond will appreciate in value. Not only could you lock in bonds that are 2, 3, even 4 percent, they will appreciate when deflation sets in and those yields go back down. Your gains could be 30 percent, 40 percent or higher over the next few years. But note: these long-term bond yields have been going down since 1981 with falling inflation—which models have been predicting. Deflation in the downturn should bring the lowest bond yields yet: under 1 percent for the 30-year Treasury bond and under 0.5 percent for the 10-year. When we see stocks looking like a bottom around 2022 or so and such low yields, you sell those bonds at a large profit and start getting back into stocks and risk assets, including higher-yield bonds, India and Southeast Asia, and industries for the aging in the U.S., like pharmaceuticals, vitamins, skin care, nursing homes, and cruise ships.

As for the dollar, once the worst of the crisis hits and the dollar has gone up 20–30 percent, back off of that. It's only good in a great crisis. The dollar is not going go up forever, but it'll do the best in the next intense crisis, which I think will last into something like late 2022 or so.

Real estate is the last thing I want to talk about; as I've already pointed out, people are emotional about real estate. People always think their real estate's special. They think their property, or city, is unique, and the bubble won't burst. But it will burst. If you live in Omaha and it hasn't bubbled up, like Dallas in the last bubble, it won't go down that much. Note that even Dallas and Denver have bubbled up more this time around.

Let me tell you how to assess your real-estate risk. This is not perfect, but since real estate is much more variable and differs greatly by region, and bubbles burst at different times than stocks, look at your real estate, whether it's a commercial or residential property. Find out what it was worth in January 2000 and what's it worth now. The January 2000 price is your minimum downside target. That's how far this bubble could go down, whether it takes two years or five. Are you willing to take that sort of loss? If that calculation comes up to only 10–20 percent, you may just want to stay in your home. Then look at what it was worth in 2012, at the last bottom. That is likely your best-case scenario.

Sell all nonstrategic discretionary real estate, especially vacation homes and investment properties, unless the cash flow is really strong, and look to rebuy later. If you can rent out your property at good positive cash flow, that is a sign that it is not as overvalued (and vice versa). You're going to be able to buy a much better vacation home if you sell what you have now (or refrain from buying in) and if you wait for years until it goes back down to those early 2000 prices. Since bubbles can go further, the 1996 or 1997 level is my next stop. That's the very worst case for real estate, but it is less likely.

Your kids are going to want to buy real estate, because most people buy their first homes between their late twenties and early thirties. If your kids are in that age range, do not let them buy a house, even if it's in foreclosure, unless it's a really super deal in an area that didn't bubble up too much. (But if it's a foreclosure, it probably did bubble up too much.) Keep them from buying real estate until at least 2023 (2025–2026 would be even better), so it's better for them to rent until then. There are a lot of advantages to renting. You free up cash flow, so you have more money to invest when things go down, and you're not tied to a house or condo that could be very hard to sell. In a downturn, real estate quickly becomes illiquid. If you don't own and a better job opportunity comes up, you can move.

Again, hang on to cash and cash-flow assets, and get into the U.S. dollar through dollar funds or UUP, and indirectly through long-term Treasury bonds. Decide if you want to be short to some percentage in order to benefit from the downturn and earn money when it goes down. Remember, stocks go down twice as fast as they bubble.

The odds are in your favor if you can get out of most real estate. I have been renting my primary home since I moved to Tampa in late 2005, when in my newsletter I was telling people the real-estate bubble was getting ready to burst, and nobody believed me. I've been renting ever since. My wife wasn't happy at first. She's very happy now. We avoided massive losses, and our rent has been half of what our mortgage and property costs would have been. So we save money and cash flow in a long-term downturn.

You may or may not want to sell your house. If you're going to stay in it forever, fine, but if you're thinking of downsizing because you're getting closer to retirement, don't wait until you're 63 or 65 or move to Arizona. Downsize now. By selling your bigger house now and converting to a house maybe half the size, you're going to cut your exposure to real-estate decline in half. A smaller house or a vacation house is also going depreciate less than big homes. The McMansions and the large homes bubble up the most. They were most in demand in the last bubble, and they're going to burst the most.

So look at your real estate from head to toe; look at all of your financial assets. It's time to restructure them now.

Next let me talk about business strategies for the winter season. When everything shakes out and gets volatile, there are a lot of entrepreneurial opportunities for people who have businesses, own their own businesses, or are looking to get into business. The nimble and quick entrepreneurs do the best and take advantage of opportunities. Other businesses will decide, "We have to get out of this business," and then there'll be a whole group of customers that are not being served. You can come in on lower overhead and take advantage of the situation if you can move and if you have cash and cash flow.

The economy has its own internal logic, just as your body does. It knows how to grow and heal and detox. This is a detox season. This is a time of bubbles bursting. It's taking massive innovations, shaking them down to the ones that really deserve to survive, and then shifting market share to those companies. That's what happened to General Motors. Ford beat them during the boom of the 1920s, but General Motors had better financial controls, better understanding of demographics, and an array of trade-up models. They got stronger in the subsequent downturn, while Ford got weaker. Ford never caught up with GM from the forties afterwards.

Identify what you're the best at and which markets you can dominate, because if you're not the best and you cannot dominate, this is going to be a survival-of-the-fittest challenge. You will lose that sector, somebody else will take it over, or the business will fail and you'll have to sell it at bargain prices. Get rid of it now in exchange for cash and cash flow. If you sell a product line that isn't dominant to some company that can dominate it, and you get X amount of dollars, that's a treasure chest. You can use it to strengthen and protect your core business, where you *can* be dominant. It's a matter of strategic focus.

When you've determined what you do best, then you have to cut costs. You have to stop spending money. You don't want to build a new factory, buy a new store, or get a new warehouse. Wait until everything's cheaper and your cash flow has grown. Cut your overheads. Both at Bain & Company and when I was with smaller businesses, the first thing I would do with any business, boom or bust, would be to come in, analyze, and separate their variable from their fixed costs.

Variable costs are easy. These are the things that you have to spend money on every time you produce or ship out another product. It's the fixed costs, the overhead, where you will find most of the waste, because it builds up bureaucratically and nobody knows how to analyze it. You have to determine how much of your fixed costs are eaten up by every department. Fixed costs include your real estate, office costs, the accounting department, the management team. You have to determine how much each of your businesses accounts for those costs, how much they use of real estate, management time, and

other resources. It'll different for every different department or category of overhead. If you
do this, you can see which products and services
account for the fixed costs. You'll see who's incurring the variable costs, and you can decide where
you break even and which businesses are losing
money.

At Bain & Company, we always came up with
major surprises. We'd allocate the overhead and
the waste and find out which divisions are losing
or making money.

That's how you shift to where you're strong.
You have to know your costs. You have to separate fixed costs from variable costs. You have to
cut those fixed costs. That's where the greatest
cost cutting is. I find that most companies can cut
overhead anywhere from 20 to 50 percent. You
know how much difference that makes? It's the
fixed costs that kill you, because when your sales
decline, your variable costs go down, but you're
still incurring your fixed costs. Your goal should
be to take over the best assets of your competitors by being one of the survivors.

Again, if you focus on what you do best, get
lean and mean, and cut costs, you're going to be
one of the survivors, because a couple of com-

panies are going to survive even if four or five go under. You want to be one of the survivors.

Most businesses and businesspeople know who their weakest competitors are and where they're weak. Identify your weak competitors. What do you want to get from them when they fail? You may contribute to their failure because you're so strong, even if you don't intend for them to fail. If they're weak, they're going to fail. Ask yourself, which of their customer segments do I want? Which key employees of theirs would I like to have? What are their technology systems? What capacity do they have that I may be able to take over in their bankruptcy at 10 or 20 cents on the dollar? You could get warehouses, stores, and production equipment for practically nothing. If you see this in advance, and if you build cash and cash flow by cutting costs, getting lean, and selling off unproductive assets, you're going to be able to come in on a moment's notice, and you're going to be able to move fast. When these companies go into bankruptcy, there's going to be a short period of time for you to zoom in and say, "I can take over these assets. Give them to me, because I have cash flow and I can pay 40 percent of their mortgage on that property."

If you can do that, the bank will be ecstatic, because the old company could only pay 10 or even zero percent. You might also be able to take over your competitor's facilities at very reasonable amounts: the bank won't have anybody else to sell them to. But you have to move cash and cash flow, and you have to think in advance, "What do I want, and from whom?"

Think of what I said before about your different products and services, especially if they're in consumer markets. Down the line, everything is tied into consumer markets—manufacturers feed wholesalers, who feed retailers. Even if you're not a retailer or dealing with customers directly, your products go to different customer segments. Which of these segments are going to be favored by demographic trends, and which are going to be disadvantaged? If you know you're in a sector that's not only going to be threatened by the downturn in the economy, but are in a sector like auto sales, which are going to get crushed, sell that business now. Sell now, and redirect your assets into areas that will do well: RVs, health care, vitamins, pharmaceuticals, or nursing homes. If you go into industries that will profit from demographics, trends are going to be more in your favor.

If you're thinking of selling your business down the road because you're going to retire or because your kids aren't interested in your business, sell it now, while you can get cash flow and it's worth much more. By the time you actually say, "I want to sell it now and retire," it could be worth only 10 or 20 cents on the dollar.

Like all things, your business has a life cycle. Know about that and know where you are on that life cycle; that'll tell you what you have to do next. Are you in the growth boom, about to go into shakeout? Get lean. Are you in the shakeout and about to go into the next maturity boom? Get your costs down and grow with a massive distribution.

Knowing the stage you're in will tell you what to do next, but understand that the economy has its own cycle, and it's a lot bigger than you or your business or your investments. You have to respect the economy's life cycle. This is what consultants can't do for you, nor can financial advisors or anybody else. I'm an expert in this. I can help you see the broader cycles.

Again, this is a time to hunker down, focus, and create cash and cash flow. Dominate your sector, come out a survivor, buy up financial assets, buy out your competitors in the downturn, and come out with greater gains in market share than you've had even in the boom. That's the payoff. You will succeed for decades if you do that.

Finally we get down to the most personal sectors—you and your family—life strategies for a world turned upside down. Again, even though you have your own life cycle, the economy has one too, and you have to take that into account.

Sell all noncrucial real estate now. You may keep your primary home, but if you're going to downsize, do it now. Imagine selling a home and buying a similar one for 50 percent or less a few years from now. Or imagine selling a vacation home. You don't use that much right now, but you probably would later. At that point you could buy a much better one on the beach or in a ski area after vacation homes have go down even more. You might buy it for 20 or 30 cents on the dollar in present-day terms.

When you're evaluating real estate, try to be as unemotional and detached as possible. This is the hardest thing for me to talk people into. If you really value your property and you're going to keep it forever, go ahead, but if you're going to downsize, do it earlier. Even consider renting your primary home for a period of time, as I have done.

My strategy has been unique. I needed a get-away place, because I think things could really get difficult. The one piece of real estate I did not sell was my place in the Caribbean. It's safe; it's out of the way; nobody knows about it. I'm sitting on 100,000 gallons of water under my house, and I have an incredible view. I could safely move there if the economy gets bad and there's more civil unrest. Besides, I might decide to retire early and move there, or I might decide to go there at certain periods.

Look at your real estate, your life, and your goals. What is strategically vital to you, and what is not? Look at your business real estate. Is your office strategically advantageous for your business? Lease it instead of owning it. That frees up cash flow. If you can sell it, you create cash flow.

You can also sell investment real estate, even if it has decent cash flow, and create a treasure chest of money. That's going to be like gold in this deflationary downturn, with the greatest sale in financial assets in history. Again, don't let your kids buy a home. They should optimally wait until later in this decade.

Instead of buying your next car, lease it, and let the dealer take the loss when you drop it off. My last few cars were worth less when I dropped them off, and I was glad I leased them. I also lease, because it's easier for tax and business reasons.

Where you live is also important. If your kids have left the nest and you're thinking about retiring or moving, either to the exurbs or into the city, consider some general principles. In the exurbs, prices are less bubbly and expensive and there's less population density. There's likely to be less of a bust here—fewer economic problems and less civil unrest. It's that simple. The greater the bust, the more foreclosures, the more unemployment, the more homeless, the more problems there are going to be.

To look at the country as a whole, instead of living on the coasts, consider living inland, especially between the two mountain ranges, the Appalachians on the east and the Rocky Mountains. As a rule, that whole inland area didn't bubble up as much, has a lower population density, and will be safer and have less unrest.

If you're looking at retiring to a nice vacation town or a college town, which is safer but where there's still a good quality of life, do it now. If you can move to a smaller town rather than a bigger one, that's going to be better.

Have a getaway plan. As I told you earlier, I have one. Where would you go, even if it's just a cabin you can rent somewhere? I don't know how bad it's going to get, because this is an unprecedentedly extreme bubble, but have some stored water, food, and other basics, as well as merchandise you can barter with.

Do I really want gold Krugerrands? First of all, gold's going to fall. It's going to fall to around $700 at worst or a new low around $1,000 at best in this next crash, by 2022 or so. Gold will keep falling, because it's a hedge against inflation, not against deflation. Besides, what can you buy with Krugerrands?

If I want to have something for barter, I'd rather have silver coins, which are more tradable and which I could actually buy a loaf of bread with. Have food and basic provisions stored. If you want to have things you can trade, what are people are going to want? Things like shotgun shells or bottles of bourbon. Just think of the things that people would really want if times got bad and you had to trade with them. If you're in a safer, more remote area, that may be less important. If you are in a more urban area, where there could be higher crime, worry about that more.

Let's get to other things. Suze Ormond and other financial experts will tell you to pay off all your debt. I say, pay off high-interest debt, like credit cards, which can be as much as 22 percent—that's crazy—but do not pay off debts with lower interest, 3 to 6 percent, such as a tax-deductible mortgage loan, because that would drain your cash.

Remember, we're looking at all levels. In personal investment and business, create cash and cash flow. That's what will most help you survive and take advantage of the great deflation and the consequent asset sale. If you pay off your mortgage just to save 3 or 4 percent interest (and which, adjusted for tax savings, might even be much less than that), you're draining your treasure chest of cash.

If you have a lot of equity in your house, that's the best reason for selling it, as you will free up the most cash to reinvest in the "sale of a lifetime" on financial assets ahead. People say, "Harry, my home is mostly paid for, so I don't have to worry about the bank taking it." No: you have the most capital stored in your home. You're the one that gets the biggest treasure chest if you sell now and buy a similar home later.

If you have a house that has, say, a $400,000 mortgage and is only worth $300,000 now and could be worth $200,000 or less, I think there's a good chance (although I can't guarantee this) that at some point the government's going to have to do the opposite of what they've done. Last time they protected the banks. They told the banks, "Don't write down loans and mortgages to market."

When the banks fail for a second time, nobody will want to bail them out again. At some point, the government's going to say to the banks, "You have to write down these mortgages for businesses and consumers." So if you're underwater, you may get a free gift. That $400,000 loan on that $300,000 house that ends up worth $200,000 may be written down to a market value of $200,000, so you may just see $200,000 of debt disappear.

Finally, let's look at your kids. If you have kids that are going to go to college or get a graduate degree, it's just common sense to say that educa-

STRATEGIES FOR THE WINTER SEASON   133

tion costs have gone up astronomically. It's seen
the highest inflation. It's way worse than health
care, and health care is a little worse than child
care.

These are the three things killing each generation: The young generation is being killed by
education costs, student loans, and child care,
which can be close to $1,000 a month. That's hor-
rible. The retiring baby boomers are being killed
by runaway health-care costs.

When this bubble bursts, everybody will
have reduced costs. The strongest will survive,
and the special interests will be in trouble. We're
going to see these bubbles burst. Costs for college
and education are only going to go down. In a
downturn, jobs are harder to get. So if your kids
are going to get higher education, it's best to do it
in the downturn. I would say your kids should
come out of school between late 2022 and mid-
2023, when the economy likely starts to recover
and turn back up. If they get out in 2021 or early
2022, they have very low chance of getting a job;
we think trends are going to be the worst then.
That's when we move into a broader, more global
boom, where our most important basic indicators start to turn up. There will be booms and

busts after that, but that's the next sustained global boom period, between 2023 and 2036. Good jobs will be available, you'll be able to invest again and to buy and hold, and your business will be able to grow without having to worry about a huge shakeout.

As I said earlier, you won't miss much if I'm wrong about specific timing. At this point, stocks and real estate are so overvalued that you'd be lucky to break even in the long run, and you'll suffer major losses in between. I may be a little early and my projections may be a little high or low, but I've never been wrong about major turning points in the economy. This is what I do. This is my unique area of expertise, and the science keeps suggesting that this is happening fast.

Remember that I have a free daily newsletter called *Economy and Markets*, which you can get at harrydent.com. It's high in content and will keep you up with what we're thinking about current events; you can sign up for it at harrydent.com/newsletter.

If you need more, we have very inexpensive newsletters at dentresearch.com that are geared to more specific needs. I used to have expensive newsletters, but I want to reach more and more people, so now I have paid newsletters that get into more detailed strategies and cost less than $100 a year. They're unbelievably affordable compared to what I've charged in the past. I want to help more people get through this coming crisis.

Look out also for my next book, *Be Your Own Boss: How to Prosper in the Coming Entrepreneurial Decade*. It will help the serious business owner who wants not only to survive and increase market share in this coming downturn, but to come roaring into the next spring season.

About the Author

Harry S. Dent, Jr. is the founder of Dent Research, an economic-research firm specializing in demographic trends. His mission is "helping people understand change."

Using exciting new research developed from years of hands-on business experience, Mr. Dent offers unprecedented and refreshingly under-standable tools for seeing the key economic trends that will affect your life, your business,

and your investments over the rest of your lifetime.

Mr. Dent is also a best-selling author. In his
book *The Great Boom Ahead* (1992), he stood vir-
tually alone in accurately forecasting the unan-
ticipated boom of the 1990s and the continued
expansion into 2007. In his recent book, *The
Demographic Cliff* (2014), he continued to educate audiences about his predictions for the next
great depression, which he has been forecasting
now for twenty years. Mr. Dent is the editor of
The Economy and Markets, *Boom-and-bust*, and *The
Leading Edge* newsletters, and he is the creator of
the Dent Network.

Mr. Dent received his MBA from Harvard
Business School, where he was a Baker Scholar
and was elected to the Century Club for leadership excellence. At Bain & Company, he was
a strategy consultant for Fortune 100 companies. He has also been the CEO of several
entrepreneurial-growth companies and has
been a new-venture investor. Since 1988, he
has been speaking to executives and investors
around the world. He has appeared on *Good
Morning America*, PBS, CNBC, CNN, and Fox and

has been featured in *Barron's*, *Investor's Business Daily*, *Entrepreneur*, *Fortune*, *SUCCESS*, *U.S. News and World Report*, *Business Week*, *The Wall Street Journal*, *American Demographics*, *Gentlemen's Quarterly*, and *Omni*.

CPSIA information can be obtained
at www.ICGtesting.com
Printed in the USA
LVHW081026020321
680301LV00001B/1